THE ULTIMATE TOWER AIR FRYER COOKBOOK UK

1200 Days Delicious and Easy Recipes to Revolutionize Your Cooking and Make Healthy Meals a Breeze, Perfect for Busy People to Make at Home

AMY H. ANDERSEN

Copyright© 2023 By Amy H. Andersen Rights Reserved

This book is copyright protected. It is only for personal use. You cannot amend, distribute, sell, use, quote or paraphrase any part of the content within this book, without the consent of the author or publisher.

Under no circumstances will any blame or legal responsibility be held against the publisher, or author, for any damages, reparation, or monetary loss due to the information contained within this book, either directly or indirectly.

Disclaimer Notice:

Please note the information contained within this document is for educational and entertainment purposes only. All effort has been executed to present accurate, up to date, reliable, complete information. No warranties of any kind are declared or implied. Readers acknowledge that the author is not engaged in the rendering of legal, financial, medical or professional advice. The content within this book has been derived from various sources. Please consult a licensed professional before attempting any techniques outlined in this book.

By reading this document, the reader agrees that under no circumstances is the author responsible for any losses, direct or indirect, that are incurred as a result of the use of the information contained within this document, including, but not limited to, errors, omissions, or inaccuracies.

EDITOR: LYN	**INTERIOR DESIGN: FAIZAN**
COVER ART: ABR	**FOOD STYLIST: JO**

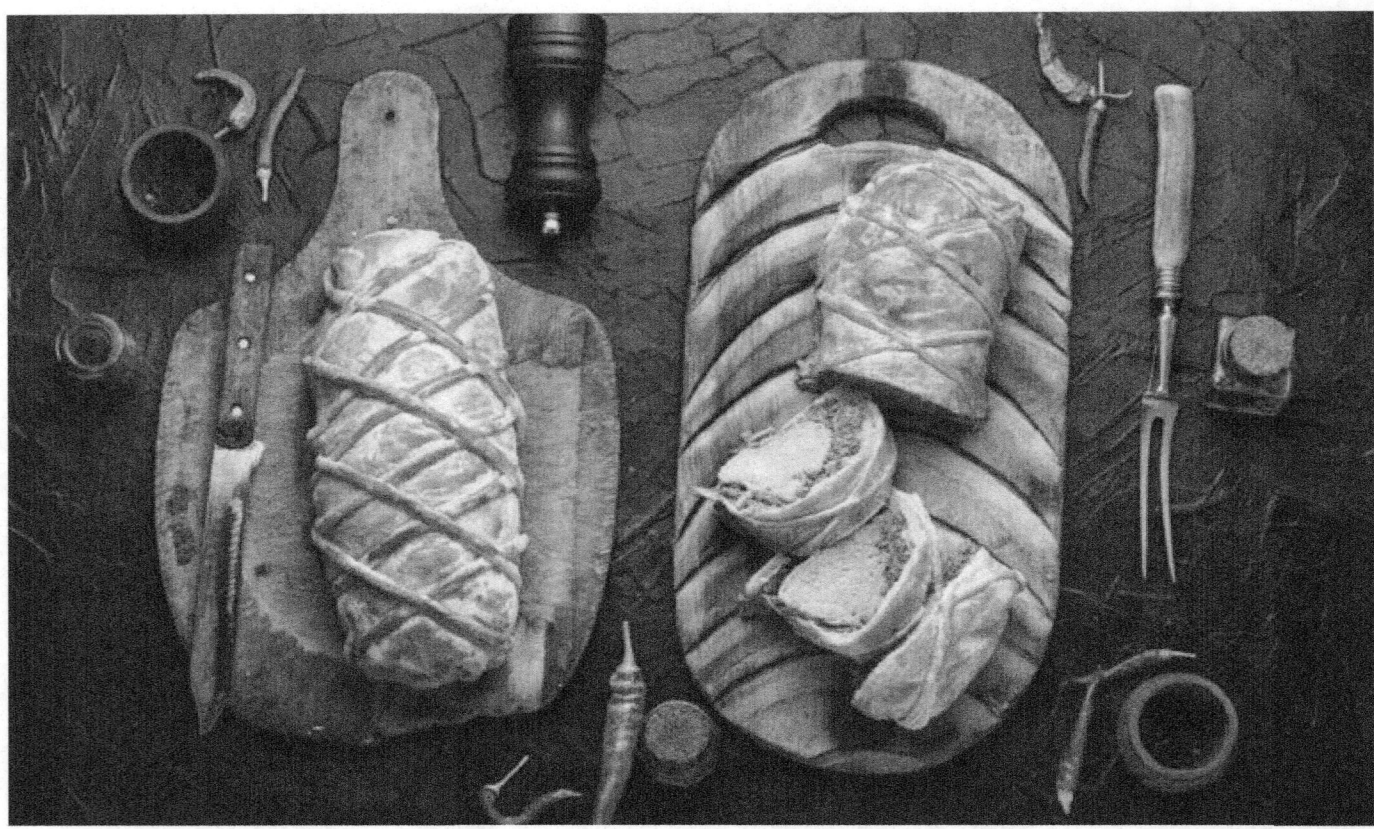

Table of Contents

Introduction	1
Chapter 1	
Getting the Most Out of Your Air Fryer	2
Tower Air Fryer Accessories	3
Advantages of Using Tower Air Fryer	3
Tower Air Fryer vs. Other Air Fryers	4
Chapter 2	
Elevate Your Air Frying	5
How to Use Tower Air Fryer	6
Maintenance and Care	7
Frequently Asked Questions	8
Air Fryer Cooking Chart	9
Chapter 3	
Breakfast Recipes	11
Spinach Eggs	12
Cauliflower Frittata	12
Omelet with Herbs de Provence	12
Tender Muffins	12
Ground Pork Casserole	13
Paprika Egg Cups	13
Swiss Chard Bake	13
Garlic Courgette Spread	13
Chilies Casserole	14
Tomato Omelet	14
Avocado Spread	14
Turkey Bake	14
Mozzarella Eggs	15
Cream Cheese Rolls	15
Avocado Bake	15
Roasted Tomato and Cheddar Rolls	15
Roasted Vegetable Frittata	16
Kale Mix	16
Western Frittata	16
Mozzarella Balls	16
Chapter 4	
Side and Snack Recipes	17
Turmeric Cauliflower Rice	18
Coconut Brussel Sprouts	18
Green BLT	18
Rutabaga Chips	18
Turmeric Cauliflower PopcornA	19
Cheese Courgette Chips	19
Keto Cauliflower "Macaroni" and Cheese	19
Creamy Cauliflower	19
Aubergine Mash	20
Nutmeg and Dill Ravioli	20
Cumin Brussels Sprouts	20
Courgette and Tomato Salsa	20
Tomato Salad	20
Cheesy Asparagus	21
Bacon Rolls	21
Garlic Chicory and Spring Onions	21
Chocolate Bacon Bites	21
Creamy Broccoli and Cauliflower	22
Parsley Cauliflower Puree	22
Coconut Celery and Broccoli Mash	22
Almond Coconut Granola	22
Cabbage Steaks	23

Coconut Chicken Bites	23
Charred Shishito Peppers	23
Crispy Spiced Chickpeas	24
Buffalo Wings	24
Goat Cheese Cauliflower and Bacon	25
Almond Broccoli Rice	25

Chapter 5
Poultry Recipes — 26

Kebab Skewers with Chicken & Tzatziki	27
Chicken and Rice Casserole	27
Chicken Wings and Vinegar Sauce	28
Gai Yang Chicken	28
Smoked Paprika Chicken	28
Asian Chicken Salad	29
Tomato Chicken Drumsticks	29
Coconut Turkey and Spinach Mix	29
Keto Chicken Cauliflower Casserole	30
Cinnamon Chicken Wings	30
Chicken Cauliflower Casserole with Pesto	30
Ginger Turkey and Cherry Tomatoes	31
Low-carb Pesto Chicken Roulade	31
Philly Chicken Cheesesteak Stromboli	31
Tortilla Crusted Chicken Breast	32
Stuffed Chicken Breast Fillet	32
Chicken Thighs with Vegetables	32
Chicken Cordon Bleu	33
Beef Steak with Broccoli	33
Chicken Breast with Arugula & Tomatoes	34
Chicken Breast with Air Fryer Vegetables	34
Chicken Breast with Peppered Vegetables	34
Chicken Breast with Green Beans	34

Chapter 6
Meat Recipes — 35

Pork and Peppers Mix	36
Hot Pork Belly	36
Dill Beef and Artichokes	36
Lamb with Paprika Cilantro Sauce	36
Apple Cornbread Stuffed Pork Loin	37
Fresh Garden Salad with Beef	37
Smoked Pork Chops with Pickled Cabbage	38
Cinnamon Lamb Meatloaf	38
Pork Schnitzel with Dill Sauce	38
Spicy Lamb Sirloin Steak	39
Beef Pot Roast	39
Creamy Pork Schnitzel	39
Beef Steak with Arugula Cherry Tomatoes	39
Sweet Pork Belly	40
Beef, Lettuce and Cabbage Salad	40
Fried Egg & Bacon	40
Keto Pork Ribs	40
Keto Mini Burger	40

Chapter 7
Fish and Seafood Recipes — 41

Balsamic Cod	42
Salmon and Lime Sauce	42
Lemon Prawn and Courgettes	43
Parmesan and Garlic Trout	43
Shrimp Spiesse	44
Chili Squid Rings	44
Trout with Herbs de Provance	45
Grilled Salmon with Green Beans	45
Parmesan Mackerel	46
Salmon Cheese Air Fryer Cakes	46
Spicy Fish Street Tacos	47
Trout and Tomato Courgette Mix	47
French Clams	47
Salmon In Zucchini Bed	48
Zoodles with Shrimp & Cherry Tomatoes	48
Tuna with Vegetables & Avocado	49
Fried Crawfish	49
Mint Sardines	49
Garlic Fish and Balsamic Salsa	50
Tender Salmon	50
Roasted Tilapia	50
Lime Lobster Tail	51
Salmon, Egg & Parmesan Salad	51

Chapter 8
Vegetable Recipes — 52

Mozzarella Asparagus Mix	53
Cheesy Green Patties	53
Green Beans and Tomato Sauce	54
Colorful Vegetable & Chicken Skewers	54
Chives Lemon Chicory Mix	55
Vegetable Spring Rolls	55
Chickpea tomato & cucumber salad	56
Kabocha Chips	56
Blooming Buttery Onion	57
Garlicky Vermouth Mushrooms	57
Chickpea & Halloumi Salad	58
Steamed Veggies	58
Chard, Avocado, Nut & Feta Salad	59
Colorful Vegetable Salad	59
Zucchini Chips	60
Sweet Pear, Pomegranate & Nuts Salad	60
Smoothie Bowl with Spinach, Mango & Muesli	61
Avocado & Mozzarella Salad Bowl	61

Chapter 9
Dessert Recipes — 62

Brownies	63
Keto Butter Balls	63
Avocado Cream Pudding	64
Walnuts and Almonds Granola	64
Cookies With Keto Marmalade	64
Tasty Potatoes Au Gratin	64
Hazelnut Vinegar Cookies	65
Keto Chocolate Mousse	65
Glazed Cherry Turnovers	66
Fresh Cucumber Salad with Onions & Herbs	66
Mediterranean Vegetable Omelet	67
Double Chocolate Cookies	67
Coconut Chocolate Fat Bombs	68
Keto Air Fryer Cakes	68
Low-Carb Carrot Cake	68
Keto Chocolate Cake	69
Lime Mousse	69

Appendix 1 Measurement Conversion Chart	70
Appendix 2 The Dirty Dozen and Clean Fifteen	71
Appendix 3 Index	72

Introduction

Air fryers have become very popular and many people have purchased one for their homes. In fact, according to a report by grand view research, the global air fryer market size was valued at usd 755.3 million in 2020 and is expected to grow at a compound annual growth rate (cagr) of 12.5% from 2021 to 2028.

Air fryers use Rapid Air Technology, which circulates hot air around the food, creating a crispy exterior while keeping the inside moist and tender. This technology allows you to achieve a fried-like texture and taste without the need for oil, or with very little oil, resulting in a healthier meal.

In addition to being a healthier cooking option, air fryers are also very versatile. They can be used to cook a wide range of foods, from chicken wings and French fries to fish, vegetables, and even desserts. Some air fryers also come with additional features, such as baking and grilling functions, making them a versatile addition to any kitchen.

Finally, air fryers are also very convenient to use. They typically require minimal preparation, and you can cook food straight from the freezer. They also have adjustable temperature controls and timers, allowing you to set the cooking time and temperature for different types of food.

Tower air fryers are also popular among consumers due to their unique features and benefits. Tower air fryers are known for their compact design, which makes them ideal for small kitchens or for those who have limited countertop space. Despite their compact size, tower air fryers can still cook a variety of foods, including chicken, fish, vegetables, and even desserts.

Tower air fryers offer a range of benefits and features that make them a popular choice among consumers who are looking for healthier, more convenient, and versatile cooking options.

Chapter 1
Getting the Most Out of Your Air Fryer

Tower Air Fryer Accessories

Tower Air Fryer is a popular kitchen appliance that allows you to cook your favorite foods with little to no oil, resulting in healthier meals. Here are some of the most common accessories that you can use with your Tower Air Fryer to enhance its functionality:

1. Grill Pan - The grill pan is usually made of non-stick material and is designed to fit perfectly inside the air fryer basket. It has raised ridges that create grill marks on the food and help drain excess fat. You can use the grill pan to cook meats, fish, and vegetables, giving your food that delicious grilled flavor without the need for an outdoor grill.
2. Baking Tray - The baking tray is also made of non-stick material and is designed to fit inside the air fryer basket. It is typically used for baking desserts, such as cakes, brownies, and cookies, but can also be used for cooking pizzas, quesadillas, and other similar foods. The baking tray is usually deeper than the standard air fryer basket, allowing you to cook larger portions of food.
3. Silicone Mat - The silicone mat is designed to be placed on the bottom of the air fryer basket. It is made of heat-resistant, non-stick material and helps prevent food from sticking to the basket. It also makes cleaning up your air fryer a breeze, as you can simply remove the mat and wash it in the sink or dishwasher.
4. Skewer Rack - The skewer rack is designed to hold multiple skewers at once, allowing you to cook a large amount of food at the same time. It typically fits inside the air fryer basket and is perfect for cooking kebabs, chicken wings, and other skewered foods. The skewer rack helps ensure that the food cooks evenly and that all sides get crispy and delicious.
5. Pizza Pan - The pizza pan is designed to fit inside the air fryer basket and is perfect for cooking pizzas. It typically has a perforated surface that allows air to circulate, creating a crispy crust. The pizza pan is also non-stick, making it easy to remove the pizza once it is cooked.
6. Multi-Layer Rack - The multi-layer rack is designed to fit inside the air fryer basket and allows you to cook multiple foods at once. It typically has multiple layers or tiers, allowing you to stack different foods on top of each other. This accessory is perfect for cooking vegetables, meats, and other similar foods, as it allows you to cook everything at the same time and saves you time in the kitchen.

Advantages of Using Tower Air Fryer

Deep-frying is a cooking method that involves submerging food in hot oil, which can result in food that is crispy and delicious but also high in calories and unhealthy fats. Consuming too much fried food has been linked to health problems such as obesity, high blood pressure, and heart disease.

On the other hand, air fryers use a technology that circulates hot air around the food, cooking it from all sides and creating a crispy texture similar to deep-fried food. However, air fryers use a tiny fraction of the oil needed for deep-frying, which means that the food is lower in calories and fat. This makes air frying a healthier alternative to deep-frying.

For example, a traditional serving of French fries contains about 340 calories and 17 grams of fat when deep-fried in oil, whereas the same serving of French fries cooked in an air fryer contains only about 140 calories and 5 grams of fat. This demonstrates the significant difference in the calorie and fat content of the same food when cooked using different methods.

An air fryer is a small, compact kitchen appliance that uses a circulating fan to cook food with hot air. Because of its compact size, an air fryer can preheat very quickly, usually in just two or three minutes. This is a huge advantage over traditional ovens or stovetops, which can take much longer to preheat.

The quick preheating time of an air fryer saves both time and energy. With a traditional oven, for example, you would need to wait for 10-15 minutes or even longer for it to preheat to the desired temperature. This not only wastes time, but it also wastes energy as the oven needs to be on for an extended period of time before you can start cooking.

In contrast, an air fryer's quick preheating time means that you can start cooking your food almost immediately, which saves time and energy. This is especially useful for busy households or those who want to cook meals quickly without having to wait for the oven or stovetop to heat up.

In addition, the quick preheating time also means that you can use the air fryer for smaller cooking jobs without having to heat up a large oven or stovetop, which can save even more time and energy. This makes the air fryer a convenient and efficient kitchen appliance that can help you cook meals quickly and easily, without wasting time or energy.

AIR-FRYING IS CONSIDERED SAFER AND EASIER THAN DEEP-FRYING FOR SEVERAL REASONS:

1. No hot oil: When deep-frying, you need to heat a large amount of oil in a pot or deep fryer, which can be dangerous. Hot oil can splatter, causing burns or fires. With an air fryer, there is no need for hot oil, so you eliminate the risk of oil-related accidents.
2. No need for monitoring: When deep-frying, you need to constantly monitor the oil temperature and the food to ensure that it is cooked evenly. This can be time-consuming and requires close attention. With an air fryer, you simply set the temperature and time, and the appliance does the rest. There is no need for constant monitoring, which makes it easier and more convenient.
3. No messy cleanup: Deep-frying can create a mess with oil splatters, and it can be difficult to clean up. With an air fryer, there is no oil to clean up, so it is much easier to clean. The removable components of an air fryer can be washed in a dishwasher or by hand, making cleanup quick and easy.

Tower Air Fryer vs. Other Air Fryers

Tower Air Fryer is one of many brands of air fryers available on the market. While there are many similarities between different air fryer brands, there are some key differences that set Tower Air Fryer apart from other air fryers.

1. Capacity: Tower Air Fryer comes in a variety of sizes, ranging from 1.5 liters to 4.3 liters. This means you can choose the size that best fits your needs. Other air fryer brands may not offer as much variety in terms of size.
2. Power: Tower Air Fryer has a wattage range of 1000-1700 watts, depending on the model. This allows for efficient and fast cooking. Other air fryer brands may have different wattage ranges, which can impact cooking time and efficiency.
3. Design: Tower Air Fryer has a sleek and modern design that can fit in with any kitchen decor. Some other air fryer brands may have bulkier or less aesthetically pleasing designs.
4. Accessories: Tower Air Fryer comes with a variety of accessories, such as a baking tray, a frying basket, and a grill rack. These accessories make it easier to cook a variety of foods and make the most of your air fryer. Other air fryer brands may not include as many accessories or may require you to purchase them separately.
5. Price: Tower Air Fryer is priced competitively compared to other air fryer brands. Depending on the model and size, the price can range from affordable to more expensive. Other air fryer brands may have different price points.

In summary, while there are many similarities between different air fryer brands, Tower Air Fryer sets itself apart through its variety of sizes, efficient power, sleek design, included accessories, and competitive pricing. Ultimately, the choice of which air fryer brand to use comes down to personal preference and the features that are most important to you.

Chapter 2
Elevate Your Air Frying

How to Use Tower Air Fryer

PREPARING TO AIR-FRY

Preparing to air-fry involves a few key steps to ensure that your food comes out delicious and evenly cooked. Here are some details on how to prepare to air-fry:

1. Choose the right food: Not all foods are suitable for air-frying. Air fryers work best with foods that are dry and have a surface that can crisp up, such as chicken, vegetables, and frozen fries. Avoid foods that are overly moist, such as soups or stews.
2. Preheat the air fryer: Preheating the air fryer helps to ensure that your food cooks evenly. Depending on your model, preheat the air fryer to the desired temperature before adding your food.
3. Prep your food: Cut your food into even pieces, and pat it dry with a paper towel to remove any excess moisture. This helps to ensure that your food crisps up properly. If you are using frozen food, let it thaw completely before cooking.
4. Season your food: Season your food with herbs, spices, or marinades to add flavor. You can also use a small amount of oil or cooking spray to help the food crisp up.
5. Arrange the food in the basket: Arrange the food in a single layer in the air fryer basket. Be sure not to overcrowd the basket, as this can affect the cooking time and quality of your food.
6. Set the time and temperature: Set the desired time and temperature according to the recipe or your preferences. Most air fryers have digital controls that allow you to set the time and temperature easily.
7. Cook the food: Close the air fryer basket and let the food cook. Depending on the food, you may need to shake the basket or turn the food over halfway through the cooking time to ensure even cooking.

WHILE YOU ARE AIR-FRYING

While you are air-frying, there are a few things to keep in mind to ensure that your food cooks evenly and comes out delicious:

1. Shake the basket: Depending on the food, you may need to shake the basket halfway through the cooking time to ensure even cooking. This helps to ensure that all sides of the food are exposed to the hot air and cook evenly.
2. Check for doneness: Check your food for doneness by using a meat thermometer or by cutting it open to check the inside. If needed, cook the food for additional time.
3. Adjust the temperature: If you find that your food is cooking too quickly or not quickly enough, you can adjust the temperature as needed. Most air fryers have adjustable temperature settings that allow you to fine-tune the cooking temperature.
4. Avoid overcrowding: Be sure not to overcrowd the air fryer basket, as this can affect the cooking time and quality of your food. Cook your food in batches if needed, rather than trying to cook everything at once.
5. Keep an eye on the food: Keep an eye on your food as it cooks, especially if you are cooking something for the first time. This can help you to adjust the cooking time or temperature as needed to ensure that your food comes out perfectly cooked.

AFTER YOU AIR-FRY, THERE ARE A FEW THINGS YOU SHOULD DO TO CLEAN AND MAINTAIN YOUR AIR FRYER:

1. Unplug the air fryer: Before cleaning your air fryer, be sure to unplug it and let it cool down completely.
2. Remove the basket: Remove the basket from the air fryer and separate any removable parts, such as the nonstick coating lining the basket, for cleaning.
3. Clean the basket and removable parts: Wash the basket and any removable parts with warm, soapy water or in the dishwasher, if they are dishwasher safe. Be sure to avoid using abrasive cleaners or metal utensils that can scratch the nonstick coating.
4. Wipe down the air fryer: Wipe down the inside and outside of the air fryer with a damp cloth or sponge. Avoid getting water inside the air fryer, as this can damage the electrical components.
5. Store the air fryer: Once the air fryer and all of its parts are completely dry, store it in a cool, dry place until the next use.

Maintenance and Care

Avoid using metal utensils: Metal utensils can scratch the nonstick coating, which can cause it to wear off over time. Instead, use silicone, wooden, or plastic utensils when cooking with your air fryer.

Use nonabrasive cleaners: When cleaning the nonstick coating, use nonabrasive cleaners and a soft sponge or cloth. Avoid using steel wool or abrasive cleaning pads, as they can scratch the nonstick coating.

Don't stack or overcrowd food: When cooking with your air fryer, avoid stacking or overcrowding food in the basket. This can cause the food to stick together and to the nonstick coating, which can damage the coating.

Use cooking spray sparingly: While some cooking sprays can be used with air fryers, it's important to use them sparingly. Excessive use of cooking spray can create a buildup that can damage the nonstick coating over time.

Avoid using harsh detergents: When cleaning the nonstick coating, avoid using harsh detergents or chemicals that can damage the coating. Stick to mild dish soap and warm water for everyday cleaning.

It is recommended to clean your air fryer after each use to maintain its performance, ensure food safety, and prolong its lifespan. Here are some steps you can follow to clean your air fryer:

1. Unplug the air fryer and let it cool down completely before cleaning.
2. Remove the basket and any other removable parts from the air fryer.

3. Wash the basket and any other removable parts with warm water and mild dish soap. You can also use a non-abrasive sponge or brush to remove any stuck-on food.
4. Wipe down the interior and exterior of the air fryer with a damp cloth. If there are any tough spots, you can use a non-abrasive sponge or brush with a small amount of dish soap.
5. Dry all parts thoroughly with a clean towel or let them air dry before reassembling the air fryer.

Frequently Asked Questions

How much oil do you need to use in an air fryer?

One of the benefits of air fryers is that you can cook with very little oil or no oil at all, depending on the food. Most recipes require only a tablespoon or two of oil, if any.

How long does it take to cook food in an air fryer?

The cooking time for air-frying varies depending on the food, but most foods can be cooked in 10-20 minutes.

How do you prevent food from sticking to the air fryer basket?

To prevent food from sticking to the air fryer basket, be sure to preheat the air fryer before adding the food. You can also lightly coat the basket with cooking spray or oil before adding the food, or use a nonstick basket. Be sure to avoid using metal utensils or abrasive cleaners, which can scratch the nonstick coating.

How can I supervise my children while they use the air fryer?

Keep a close eye on your children while they are using the air fryer, especially if they are young or inexperienced with kitchen appliances. Don't leave them unattended while the air fryer is in use. You can also guide them through the process of using the air fryer, and explain the safety guidelines and precautions.

What should I teach my children about using the air fryer?

Teach your children how to properly handle and operate the air fryer. Show them how to insert and remove the basket safely, how to adjust the temperature and timer, and how to clean the air fryer after use. Also, make sure they understand the safety guidelines and precautions, such as avoiding contact with hot surfaces or splashing oil.

How can I prevent accidents while using the air fryer?

Make sure the air fryer is placed on a stable and secure surface to prevent any accidents or falls. Also, keep the air fryer away from other kitchen appliances or utensils that can cause interference or accidents. Read the user manual carefully to learn about the safety guidelines and precautions, and follow them carefully.

What should I do to avoid overcooking or burning food?

Use a timer to avoid overcooking or burning food, and set the temperature according to the recipe or food being cooked. You can also use a meat thermometer to check the internal temperature of meat or poultry to ensure it's fully cooked. Don't overcrowd the air fryer basket, as this can cause uneven cooking and burning.

How can I avoid burning my hands or fingers?

Consider using a non-slip mat or gloves to avoid burning your hands or fingers when handling hot food or the air fryer basket. You can also use a pair of tongs or a spatula to remove the food from the air fryer basket. Let the air fryer cool down before you clean it or remove the basket.

What can I do to enjoy a variety of healthy, delicious meals?

Experiment with different recipes and foods to enjoy a variety of healthy, delicious meals. You can air fry vegetables, seafood, meat, poultry, and even desserts. Try different seasonings and spices to add flavor to your food. You can also search for recipes online or in cookbooks for inspiration.

Air Fryer Cooking Chart

Food	Temperature (°C)	Cooking Time (minutes)
French fries (thin)	200	10-15
French fries (thick)	200	15-20
Chicken wings	180	20-25
Chicken breast	180	15-20
Salmon fillet	200	8-10
Shrimp	200	8-10
Onion rings	200	8-10
Vegetables (broccoli, etc.)	180	10-15
Frozen vegetables (mix)	180	10-15
Breaded fish fillets	200	10-12
Hamburgers	200	8-10
Bacon	180	6-8
Sausages	180	12-15
Meatballs	180	12-15
Baked potatoes	200	45-50
Sweet potatoes	200	20-25
Chicken breasts	200	15-20 min
Chicken thighs	200	20-25 min
Chicken wings	200	18-20 min
Fish fillets	200	8-12 min
Shrimp	200	6-8 min
Scallops	200	6-8 min
Salmon	200	10-12 min
Pork chops	200	12-15 min
Pork tenderloin	200	20-25 min
Steak (1 inch thick)	200	8-10 min
Hamburger patties	200	8-10 min
Hot dogs/sausages	200	6-8 min

Food	Temperature (°C)	Cooking Time (minutes)
French fries	200	15-20 min
Sweet potato fries	200	15-20 min
Potato wedges	200	15-20 min
Onion rings	200	12-15 min
Zucchini/squash fries	200	10-12 min
Broccoli/cauliflower	200	8-10 min
Brussel sprouts	200	12-15 min
Carrots	200	12-15 min
Asparagus	200	6-8 min
Corn on the cob	200	12-15 min
Baked potatoes	200	40-45 min
Stuffed mushrooms	200	8-10 min
Roasted peppers	200	8-10 min
Chicken nuggets	200	10-12 min
Meatballs	200	10-12 min
Spring rolls	200	10-12 min
Mozzarella sticks	200	6-8 min
Jalapeno poppers	200	8-10 min
Quiche	180	25-30 min
Puff pastry	200	10-12 min
Apple turnovers	200	12-15 min
Chocolate chip cookies	180	6-8 min

Note: Cooking times may vary depending on the type and brand of air fryer, as well as the size and thickness of the food being cooked. Always refer to the manufacturer's instructions and use a food thermometer to ensure that food is cooked to a safe temperature.

Chapter 3
Breakfast Recipes

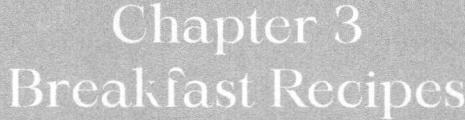

Spinach Eggs

Prep time: 8 minutes | Cook time: 20 minutes | Serves 4

- 1 tablespoon rapeseed oil
- ½ teaspoon chili flakes
- 6 eggs, beaten
- 200g spinach, chopped

1. In a mixing bowl, mix together the chili flakes, beaten eggs, and chopped spinach.
2. Brush the air fryer mold with rapeseed oil. Pour the egg mixture inside and transfer the mold into the air fryer.
3. Cook the meal at 185°C (365°F) for 20 minutes.

Cauliflower Frittata

Prep time: 10 minutes | Cook time: 14 minutes | Serves 4

- 4 eggs, beaten
- 1 tablespoon cream cheese
- 120ml double cream
- 120g cauliflower, chopped
- ½ teaspoon chili flakes
- ½ teaspoon rapeseed oil

1. In a mixing bowl, mix together the beaten eggs, cream cheese, double cream, and chili flakes.
2. Brush the air fryer basket with rapeseed oil and put the cauliflower inside. Flatten it into one layer.
3. Pour the egg mixture over the cauliflower and cook the meal at 190°C (370°F) for 14 minutes.

Omelet with Herbs de Provence

Prep time: 10 minutes | Cook time: 18 minutes | Serves 3

- 6 large eggs
- 1 tablespoon coconut milk
- 1 teaspoon Herbs de Provence
- 1 teaspoon coconut oil
- 28g Parmesan cheese, grated

1. Grease the air fryer basket with coconut oil.
2. In a mixing bowl, whisk together the eggs, coconut milk, and Herbs de Provence.
3. Pour the egg mixture into the greased air fryer basket.
4. Sprinkle grated Parmesan cheese on top of the egg mixture.
5. Air fry the omelette at 180°C (365°F) for 18 minutes or until fully cooked.
6. Once cooked, remove the omelette from the air fryer and serve hot.

Tender Muffins

Prep time: 15 minutes | Cook time: 12 minutes | Serves 4

- 4 rashers of bacon, chopped
- 4 eggs, beaten
- 60ml coconut cream
- 1 tsp dried dill
- 1 tsp softened butter or margarine
- ½ tsp chopped chives

1. Preheat the oven to 180°C/350°F/Gas Mark 4. Grease a muffin tin with butter or margarine.
2. In a mixing bowl, combine the chopped bacon, beaten eggs, coconut cream, dried dill, butter or margarine, and chopped chives. Mix well.
3. Spoon the mixture evenly into the muffin tin.
4. Bake for 12 minutes or until the muffins are firm to the touch and lightly browned.
5. Remove from the oven and let cool for a few minutes before serving.

Ground Pork Casserole

Prep time: 15 minutes | Cook time: 25 minutes |Serves 6

- 2 green chillies, sliced
- 450g ground pork
- 100g Cheddar cheese, grated
- 1 teaspoon coconut oil
- 1 teaspoon chili flakes
- 1/2 teaspoon ground turmeric

1. Grease the air fryer basket with coconut oil.
2. In a mixing bowl, combine ground pork with sliced green chillies, chili flakes, and ground turmeric.
3. Transfer the mixture to the air fryer basket and flatten it. Top with grated Cheddar cheese.
4. Cook the casserole at 190C/375F for 25 minutes.

Paprika Egg Cups

Prep time: 10 minutes | Cook time: 3 minutes |Serves 2

- 2 medium eggs
- 15g cream cheese
- 1 teaspoon smoked paprika

1. Crack the eggs into two ramekins and top with smoked paprika and cream cheese.
2. Place the ramekins in the air fryer and cook at 200°C for 3 minutes.

Swiss Chard Bake

Prep time: 10 minutes | Cook time: 15 minutes |Serves 4

- 4 eggs, beaten
- 1 tablespoon coconut cream
- 2 oz Swiss Chard, chopped
- ½ teaspoon coconut oil
- 1 oz Provolone cheese, grated

1. Grease the air fryer basket with coconut oil.
2. Then pour the beaten eggs into the basket.
3. Add coconut cream, Provolone cheese, and Swiss Chard to the eggs.
4. Air fry the mixture at 190°C (375°F) for 15 minutes, or until the eggs are firm.

Garlic Courgette Spread

Prep time: 10 minutes | Cook time: 15 minutes |Serves 4

- 4 courgettes, roughly chopped
- 1 teaspoon garlic powder
- 1 tablespoon avocado oil
- ½ teaspoon salt

1. Mix courgettes with garlic powder, avocado oil, and salt.
2. Put the mixture in the air fryer and bake at 190°C/375°F for 15 minutes.
3. Then blend the cooked courgettes until you get smooth spread.

Chilies Casserole

Prep time: 10 minutes | Cook time: 15 minutes | Serves 2

- 1 red chili pepper, chopped
- 1 cup minced chicken
- 25g Mozzarella, grated
- ½ teaspoon ground cinnamon
- ½ teaspoon coconut oil
- 25g cauliflower, chopped

1. Mix the chopped chili pepper, minced chicken, grated Mozzarella, ground cinnamon, and chopped cauliflower in a mixing bowl.
2. Grease the air fryer basket with coconut oil, and then add the mixture inside.
3. Cook the casserole in the air fryer at 190°C/375°F for 15 minutes.

Tomato Omelet

Prep time: 5 minutes | Cook time: 20 minutes | Serves 4

- 6 eggs, beaten
- 1 tomato, chopped
- 1 teaspoon coconut oil, melted
- ½ teaspoon dried dill
- ½ teaspoon salt

1. Mix eggs with dried dill and salt.
2. Grease the air fryer basket with coconut oil and pour the egg mixture inside.
3. Add chopped tomatoes and cook the omelet for 20 minutes at 185°C (365°F).

Avocado Spread

Prep time: 10 minutes | Cook time: 10 minutes | Serves 4

- 1 teaspoon garlic powder
- 1 avocado, pitted, peeled, chopped
- 1 tablespoon pork scratchings, chopped
- 1 egg
- 1 tablespoon cream cheese

1. Preheat the air fryer to 190°C/375°F.
2. Mix beaten egg with pork scratchings and pour the mixture into the air fryer.
3. Cook for 10 minutes at 196°C/385°F. Stir the cooked egg mixture well.
4. Then mix it with garlic powder, avocado, and cream cheese. Blend the mixture well.

Turkey Bake

Prep time: 10 minutes | Cook time: 25 minutes | Serves 2

- 450g ground turkey
- 2 teaspoons rapeseed oil
- 480ml coconut milk
- 100g Monterey jack cheese, grated
- 2 eggs, beaten
- 1 teaspoon ground black pepper

1. Grease the baking dish with rapeseed oil.
2. In a mixing bowl, combine ground turkey with coconut milk, cheese, eggs, and ground black pepper.
3. Transfer the mixture into the greased baking dish and flatten it gently.
4. Bake the turkey bake at 190°C (375°F) for 25 minutes.

Mozzarella Eggs

Prep time: 5 minutes | Cook time: 20 minutes | Serves 4

- 120g mozzarella, shredded
- 4 eggs
- 1 teaspoon coconut oil, softened
- ½ teaspoon ground black pepper

1. Grease the air fryer basket with coconut oil and crack the eggs inside.
2. Sprinkle the eggs with ground black pepper and mozzarella.
3. Cook the meal at 180°C (360°F) for 20 minutes.

Cream Cheese Rolls

Prep time: 15 minutes | Cook time: 10 minutes | Serves 4

- 4 eggs, beaten
- ½ teaspoon coconut oil, melted
- ½ teaspoon chili flakes
- 2 tablespoons cream cheese

1. Mix eggs with chili flakes.
2. Then brush the air fryer basket with coconut oil and preheat it to 200°C (395°F).
3. Make 4 crepes from egg mixture and cook them in the air fryer basket.
4. Then spread the cream cheese over every egg crepe and roll.

Avocado Bake

Prep time: 10 minutes | Cook time: 20 minutes | Serves 2

- 1 avocado, pitted, halved
- 2 eggs
- 1 oz Parmesan, grated
- ½ teaspoon ground nutmeg

1. Preheat the oven to 180°C/ 350°F/ Gas Mark 4.
2. Scoop out a little of the avocado flesh to make a larger hole in each half.
3. Crack one egg into each avocado half.
4. Top each egg with Parmesan and ground nutmeg.
5. Place the avocado halves on a baking sheet and bake in the preheated oven for 20 minutes until the eggs are set.

Roasted Tomato and Cheddar Rolls

Prep time: 5 minutes | Cook time: 55 minutes | Serves 12

- 4 vine-ripened tomatoes
- ½ clove garlic, minced
- 1 tablespoon olive oil
- ¼ teaspoon dried thyme
- salt and freshly ground black pepper
- 500g strong bread flour
- 1 teaspoon fast-action yeast
- 2 teaspoons sugar
- 2 teaspoons salt
- 1 tablespoon olive oil
- 100g grated Cheddar cheese, plus more for sprinkling at the end
- 350ml water

1. Cut the vine-ripened tomatoes in half, remove the seeds with your fingers and transfer to a bowl. Add the garlic, olive oil, dried thyme, salt and freshly ground black pepper and toss well.
2. Preheat the oven to 200°C/180°C fan/gas mark 6.
3. Place the tomatoes, cut side up on a baking tray and roast for 25-30 minutes until they are starting to brown and are no longer juicy. Let the tomatoes cool and then roughly chop them.
4. Combine the flour, yeast, sugar, and salt in the bowl of a stand mixer. Add the olive oil, chopped roasted tomatoes, and Cheddar cheese to the flour mixture and start to mix using the dough hook attachment. As you're mixing, add 350ml of water, mixing until the dough comes together. Continue to knead the dough with the dough hook for another 10 minutes, adding enough water to the dough to get it to the right consistency.
5. Transfer the dough to an oiled bowl, cover with a clean kitchen towel and let it rest and rise until it has doubled in volume – about 1 to 2 hours. Then, divide the dough into 12 equal portions. Roll each portion of dough into a ball. Lightly coat each dough ball with oil and let the dough balls rest and rise a second time, covered lightly with plastic wrap for 45 minutes. (Alternatively, you can place the rolls in the refrigerator overnight and take them out 2 hours before you bake them.)
6. Preheat the oven to 200°C/180°C fan/gas mark 6.
7. Spray the dough balls with a little olive oil and place them on a baking tray lined with baking parchment. Bake for 20-25 minutes until the rolls are golden brown and cooked through. Add a little grated Cheddar cheese on top of the rolls for the last 2 minutes of baking for an attractive finish.

Roasted Vegetable Frittata

Prep time: 5 minutes | Cook time: 19 minutes | Serves 1 to 2

- ½ red or green bell pepper, cut into ½-inch chunks
- 4 button mushrooms, sliced
- ½ cup diced courgette
- ½ teaspoon chopped fresh oregano or thyme
- 1 teaspoon olive oil
- 3 eggs, beaten
- ½ cup grated Cheddar cheese
- salt and freshly ground black pepper, to taste
- 1 teaspoon butter
- 1 teaspoon chopped fresh parsley

1. Pre-heat the air fryer to 200°C/400°F.
2. Toss the peppers, mushrooms, courgette and oregano with the olive oil and air-fry for 6 minutes, shaking the basket once or twice during the cooking process to redistribute the ingredients.
3. While the vegetables are cooking, beat the eggs well in a bowl, stir in the Cheddar cheese and season with salt and freshly ground black pepper. Add the air-fried vegetables to this bowl when they have finished cooking.
4. Place a 6- or 7-inch non-stick metal cake pan into the air fryer basket with the butter using an aluminum sling to lower the pan into the basket. (Fold a piece of aluminium foil into a strip about 2-inches wide by 24-inches long.) Air-fry for 1 minute at 190°C/380°F to melt the butter. Remove the cake pan and rotate the pan to distribute the butter and grease the pan. Pour the egg mixture into the cake pan and return the pan to the air fryer, using the aluminium sling.
5. Air-fry at 190°C/380°F for 12 minutes, or until the frittata has puffed up and is lightly browned. Let the frittata sit in the air fryer for 5 minutes to cool to an edible temperature and set up. Remove the cake pan from the air fryer, sprinkle with parsley and serve immediately.

Kale Mix

Prep time: 5 minutes | Cook time: 20 minutes | Serves 4

- 4 kalamata olives, chopped
- 1 cup kale, chopped
- 2 oz Cheddar cheese, grated
- 4 eggs, beaten
- ½ teaspoon smoked paprika

1. Mix all ingredients in a mixing bowl.
2. Pour the mixture into the air fryer basket.
3. Flatten the mixture and cook at 180°C (360°F) for 20 minutes.

Western Frittata

Prep time: 5 minutes | Cook time: 10 minutes | Serves 1 to 2

- ½ red or green bell pepper, cut into 1 cm chunks
- 1 teaspoon olive oil
- 3 eggs, beaten
- 25g grated Cheddar cheese
- 25g diced cooked ham
- salt and freshly ground black pepper, to taste
- 1 teaspoon butter
- 1 teaspoon chopped fresh parsley

1. Preheat the air fryer to 200°C.
2. Toss the peppers with the olive oil and air-fry for 6 minutes, shaking the basket once or twice during the cooking process to redistribute the ingredients.
3. While the vegetables are cooking, beat the eggs well in a bowl, stir in the Cheddar cheese and ham, and season with salt and freshly ground black pepper. Add the air-fried peppers to this bowl when they have finished cooking.
4. Place a 6- or 7-inch non-stick metal cake pan into the air fryer basket with the butter using an aluminium sling to lower the pan into the basket. (Fold a piece of aluminium foil into a strip about 5 cm wide by 60 cm long.) Air-fry for 1 minute at 190°C to melt the butter. Remove the cake pan and rotate the pan to distribute the butter and grease the pan. Pour the egg mixture into the cake pan and return the pan to the air fryer, using the aluminium sling.
5. Air-fry at 190°C for 12 minutes, or until the frittata has puffed up and is lightly browned. Let the frittata sit in the air fryer for 5 minutes to cool to an edible temperature and set up. Remove the cake pan from the air fryer, sprinkle with parsley and serve immediately.

Mozzarella Balls

Prep time: 15 minutes | Cook time: 12 minutes | Serves 6

- 4 tablespoons coconut flour
- 120g Mozzarella cheese, shredded
- 1 teaspoon Erythritol
- 2 tablespoons coconut oil, softened
- ¼ teaspoon baking powder
- 1 egg, beaten

1. In a mixing bowl, combine the coconut flour, shredded Mozzarella cheese, Erythritol, softened coconut oil, baking powder, and beaten egg. Knead the mixture to form a dough.
2. Shape the dough into balls and place them in the air fryer basket.
3. Cook the Mozzarella balls in the air fryer at 185°C (365°F) for 12 minutes.

Chapter 4
Side and Snack Recipes

Turmeric Cauliflower Rice

Prep time: 5 minutes | Cook time: 20 minutes | Serves 4

- 750g cauliflower, grated
- 1 tbsp coconut oil
- 1 tsp ground turmeric
- ½ tsp dried oregano

1. Grease the air fryer basket with coconut oil.
2. Mix the grated cauliflower with ground turmeric and dried oregano. Place the mixture in the air fryer.
3. Cook the cauliflower rice at 180°C for 20 minutes, shaking the rice from time to time to avoid burning.

Coconut Brussel Sprouts

Prep time: 10 minutes | Cook time: 15 minutes | Serves 4

- 227g Brussels sprouts
- 1 tablespoon desiccated coconut
- 1 tablespoon coconut oil
- 1 teaspoon ground paprika
- 1 teaspoon ground black pepper

1. Put all ingredients in the air fryer basket and toss well.
2. Cook the dish at 193C for 15 minutes. Toss the sprouts while cooking every 5 minutes to ensure even cooking.

Green BLT

Prep time: 10 minutes | Cook time: 4 minutes | Serves 4

- 2 green tomatoes (unripe)
- 25g almond flour
- 2 eggs, beaten
- 1/4 teaspoon ground black pepper
- 1/4 teaspoon chili powder
- 28g Monterey Jack cheese, shredded
- 4 lettuce leaves

1. Slice the green tomatoes into 4 slices and sprinkle with ground black pepper and chili powder.
2. Dip the tomato slices in the eggs and coat them in the almond flour. Repeat this step one more time.
3. Place the coated tomato slices in the air fryer basket and cook them at 200°C/400°F for 2 minutes per side.
4. Then, place the cooked tomato slices on the lettuce leaves and top with Monterey Jack cheese.

Rutabaga Chips

Prep time: 10 minutes | Cook time: 20 minutes | Serves 4

- 425 grams rutabaga, cut into thin slices
- 4 tablespoons avocado oil
- 1 teaspoon garlic powder

1. Toss the rutabaga slices with garlic powder and avocado oil and place them in the air fryer basket.
2. Cook the rutabaga crisps at 180C/360F for 20 minutes, shaking the basket every 5-7 minutes to ensure even cooking.
3. Once crispy and golden, remove from the air fryer and serve.

Turmeric Cauliflower PopcornA
Prep time: 10 minutes | Cook time: 11 minutes | Serves 4

- 240g cauliflower florets
- 1 teaspoon ground turmeric
- 2 eggs, beaten
- 2 tablespoons almond flour
- 1 teaspoon salt
- Cooking spray

1. Cut the cauliflower florets into small pieces and sprinkle with ground turmeric and salt.
2. Then dip the vegetables in the eggs and coat in the almond flour.
3. Preheat the air fryer to 200°C (400°F).
4. Place the cauliflower popcorn in the air fryer in one layer and cook for 7 minutes.
5. Give a good shake to the vegetables and cook them for 4 minutes more.

Keto Cauliflower "Macaroni" and Cheese
Prep time: 10 minutes | Cook time: 10 minutes | Serves 4

- 2 cups cauliflower florets, chopped
- 1 teaspoon olive oil
- 1 teaspoon salt
- 1 teaspoon dried oregano
- ½ cup Monterey Jack cheese, shredded
- ½ cup heavy cream
- ½ teaspoon coconut oil

1. Put the cauliflower in the air fryer basket.
2. Sprinkle it with avocado oil, salt, dried oregano, heavy cream, and coconut oil.
3. Then shake the mixture and top it with Monterey Jack cheese.
4. Cook the meal at 204°C (or the nearest temperature on your air fryer) for 10 minutes.

Cheese Courgette Chips
Prep time: 10 minutes | Cook time: 13 minutes | Serves 8

- 2 courgettes, thinly sliced
- 4 tablespoons almond flour
- 2 oz Parmesan
- 2 eggs, beaten
- ½ teaspoon white pepper
- Cooking spray

1. In a large bowl, mix together the almond flour, Parmesan, and white pepper.
2. Dip the courgette slices in the beaten egg and coat them in the almond flour mixture.
3. Preheat the air fryer to 180°C (355°F).
4. Place the prepared courgette slices in the air fryer in a single layer and cook them for 10 minutes.
5. Flip the vegetables over and cook them for an additional 3 minutes or until crispy.

Creamy Cauliflower
Prep time: 10 minutes | Cook time: 25 minutes | Serves 4

- 225g cauliflower florets, boiled
- 70g ground chicken
- 1 tablespoon keto tomato sauce
- 1 tablespoon coconut oil
- 2 tablespoons cream cheese
- 70g Mozzarella cheese, shredded
- 1 teaspoon fresh parsley, chopped
- 1 teaspoon salt
- 1 teaspoon cayenne pepper
- ½ teaspoon basil

1. Melt the coconut oil in a skillet over medium heat.
2. Add ground chicken, salt, cayenne pepper, and parsley. Mix well.
3. Add basil and continue to cook for 5 minutes.
4. Add tomato sauce and mix well.
5. Place half of the cauliflower florets in the air fryer basket.
6. Top the cauliflower with the ground chicken mixture.
7. Cover this layer with the remaining cauliflower, cream cheese, and Mozzarella cheese.
8. Cook the meal at 190C/375F for 10 minutes.

Aubergine Mash

Prep time: 10 minutes | Cook time: 15 minutes | Serves 4

- ½ cup Mozzarella, shredded
- 2 aubergines, trimmed
- 1 tablespoon avocado oil
- ½ teaspoon dried coriander

1. Dice the aubergines and toss them with avocado oil.
2. Cook the vegetables in the air fryer for 15 minutes.
3. Then transfer them to a blender. Add coriander and cheese.
4. Blend the mixture until smooth.

Nutmeg and Dill Ravioli

Prep time: 20 minutes | Cook time: 8 minutes | Serves 6

- 4 tablespoons ground almonds
- 2 tablespoons coconut flour
- 1 tablespoon xanthan gum
- ½ teaspoon baking powder
- 1 beaten egg
- 1 tablespoon water
- 1 teaspoon apple cider vinegar
- 4 tablespoons ricotta cheese
- ½ teaspoon minced garlic
- ¼ teaspoon ground nutmeg
- ½ teaspoon dried dill
- 1 egg yolk, whisked
- Cooking spray

1. Make the dough: mix ground almonds, coconut flour, xanthan gum, baking powder, beaten egg, water, and apple cider vinegar.
2. Knead the dough with the help of the fingertips until it is soft and non-sticky.
3. Roll out the dough and cut it into ravioli squares.
4. Make the ravioli filling: mix dried dill, ground nutmeg, minced garlic, and ricotta cheese.
5. Then fill the dough squares with ricotta cheese.
6. Top the cheese with another ravioli dough square.
7. Secure the edges.
8. Brush the ravioli with egg yolk.
9. Preheat the air fryer to 190°C (375°F).
10. Spray the air fryer basket with cooking spray and place the ravioli inside in one layer.
11. Cook the meal for 4 minutes on each side or until they are light brown.

Cumin Brussels Sprouts

Prep time: 5 minutes | Cook time: 15 minutes | Serves 4

- 454g Brussels sprouts, trimmed and shredded
- 118ml olive oil
- Juice of 1 lemon
- Zest of 1 lemon, grated
- A pinch of salt and black pepper
- 28g almonds, toasted and chopped
- 1/2 teaspoon cumin, crushed
- 1 teaspoon chili paste

1. In a pan that fits the air fryer, combine the Brussels sprouts with all the other ingredients, toss, put the pan in the fryer and cook at 200 degrees Celsius for 15 minutes.
2. Divide between plates and serve as a side dish.

Courgette and Tomato Salsa

Prep time: 5 minutes | Cook time: 15 minutes | Serves 6

- 680g courgettes, roughly cubed
- 2 spring onions, chopped
- 2 tomatoes, cubed
- Salt and black pepper to taste
- 1 tablespoon balsamic vinegar

1. In a pan that fits your air fryer, mix all the ingredients, toss, introduce the pan in the fryer and cook at 180 degrees C (360 degrees F) for 15 minutes.
2. Divide the salsa into cups and serve cold.

Tomato Salad

Prep time: 5 minutes | Cook time: 12 minutes | Serves 6

- 450g tomatoes, sliced
- 1 tablespoon balsamic vinegar
- 1 tablespoon ginger, grated
- ½ teaspoon coriander, ground
- 1 teaspoon sweet paprika
- 1 teaspoon chili powder
- 100g mozzarella, shredded

1. In a pan that fits your air fryer, mix all the ingredients except the mozzarella, toss, introduce the pan in the air fryer and cook at 180 degrees Celsius for 12 minutes.
2. Divide into bowls and serve cold as an appetizer with the mozzarella sprinkled all over.

Cheesy Asparagus

Prep time: 10 minutes | Cook time: 5 minutes | Serves 3

- 250g Asparagus
- 30g Parmesan, grated
- 5ml avocado oil

1. Trim the asparagus spears and toss with avocado oil.
2. Place them in the air fryer basket and cook at 200°C for 5 minutes.
3. Transfer the cooked asparagus to a serving plate and sprinkle with grated Parmesan.

Bacon Rolls

Prep time: 10 minutes | Cook time: 8 minutes | Serves 5

- 5 rashers of streaky bacon
- 3 tablespoons mascarpone
- 1 teaspoon dried oregano

1. Preheat the air fryer to 200°C (400°F).
2. Place the bacon rashers in the air fryer basket in a single layer and cook for 4 minutes on each side.
3. Allow the bacon to cool slightly and then sprinkle with dried oregano.
4. Spread the mascarpone over the bacon slices and roll them up.

Garlic Chicory and Spring Onions

Prep time: 5 minutes | Cook time: 20 minutes | Serves 4

- 2 spring onions, chopped
- 3 garlic cloves, minced
- 1 tablespoon olive oil
- Salt and freshly ground black pepper to taste
- 1 teaspoon chili sauce
- 4 chicory heads, trimmed and roughly shredded

1. Grease a pan that fits your air fryer with the oil, add all the ingredients, toss, introduce in the air fryer and cook at 190 degrees Celsius (370 degrees Fahrenheit) for 20 minutes.
2. Divide everything between plates and serve.

Chocolate Bacon Bites

Prep time: 5 minutes | Cook time: 10 minutes | Serves 4

- 8 rashers of bacon, halved
- 100g dark chocolate, melted
- A pinch of pink salt

1. Dip each halved bacon rasher in the melted dark chocolate, sprinkle with pink salt, and place them in the air fryer basket.
2. Preheat the air fryer to 175°C (350°F) and cook for 10 minutes.
3. Serve as a snack.

Creamy Broccoli and Cauliflower

Prep time: 5 minutes | Cook time: 20 minutes | Serves 4

- 425g broccoli florets
- 285g cauliflower florets
- 1 leek, chopped
- 2 spring onions, chopped
- Salt and black pepper to taste
- 57g butter, melted
- 2 tablespoons mustard
- 240ml sour cream
- 142g mozzarella cheese, shredded

1. Grease a baking pan that fits your air fryer with the melted butter.
2. Add the broccoli, cauliflower, leek, spring onions, salt, black pepper, and mustard to the pan and toss until everything is coated with butter and seasoning.
3. Sprinkle the shredded mozzarella cheese over the top.
4. Place the pan in the air fryer and cook at 190°C for 20 minutes.
5. Serve as a side dish.

Parsley Cauliflower Puree

Prep time: 10 minutes | Cook time: 8 minutes | Serves 2

- 350g cauliflower, chopped
- 15g butter, melted
- ½ teaspoon salt
- 1 tablespoon fresh parsley, chopped
- 60ml double cream
- Cooking spray

1. Put the cauliflower in the air fryer and spray with cooking spray.
2. Cook it for 8 minutes at 200C.
3. Stir the vegetables after 4 minutes of cooking.
4. Then preheat the heavy cream until it is hot and pour it in the blender.
5. Add cauliflower, parsley, salt, and butter.
6. Blend the mixture until you get the smooth puree.

Coconut Celery and Broccoli Mash

Prep time: 10 minutes | Cook time: 5 minutes | Serves 2

- 200g broccoli florets
- 1 tablespoon almond butter
- ½ teaspoon salt
- 60g celery stalk, chopped
- 2 tablespoons coconut cream
- Cooking spray

1. Preheat the air fryer to 200°C.
2. Then put the broccoli florets and celery stalk in the air fryer basket and spray them with cooking spray.
3. Cook the vegetables for 5 minutes at 200°C.
4. Then put the cooked vegetables in the blender and blend them until you get a puree.
5. After this, put the puree in the bowl.
6. Add salt, almond butter, and coconut cream.
7. Stir the puree with the help of the spoon.

Almond Coconut Granola

Prep time: 10 minutes | Cook time: 12 minutes | Serves 4

- 1 teaspoon agave syrup
- 1 teaspoon almond butter
- 1 teaspoon coconut oil
- 2 tablespoons almonds, chopped
- 1 teaspoon pumpkin puree
- ½ teaspoon mixed spice
- 2 tablespoons desiccated coconut
- 2 tablespoons pumpkin seeds, crushed
- 1 teaspoon hemp seeds
- 1 teaspoon flax seeds
- Cooking spray

1. In a large bowl, mix together the almond butter and coconut oil.
2. Heat the mixture in the microwave until melted.
3. In a separate bowl, mix together the agave syrup, mixed spice, desiccated coconut, pumpkin seeds, hemp seeds, and flax seeds.
4. Add the melted coconut oil and pumpkin puree to the bowl and stir until well combined.
5. Preheat the air fryer to 180°C (350°F).
6. Line a baking tray with parchment paper and shape the granola mixture into a square on the paper.
7. Cut the square into serving bars and transfer to the preheated air fryer.
8. Cook the granola for 12 minutes.

Cabbage Steaks

Prep time: 10 minutes | Cook time: 25 minutes | Serves 4

- 454g white cabbage, cut into steaks
- 1 tablespoon rapeseed oil
- 1 teaspoon salt
- 1 teaspoon apple cider vinegar
- ½ teaspoon mustard

1. Rub the white cabbage steaks with rapeseed oil, salt, apple cider vinegar, and mustard.
2. Then put them in the air fryer basket in one layer and cook at 190C for 15 minutes.
3. After this, flip the cabbage steaks on another side and cook them for 10 minutes more.

Coconut Chicken Bites

Prep time: 5 minutes | Cook time: 20 minutes | Serves 4

- 2 teaspoons garlic powder
- 2 eggs
- Salt and black pepper to taste
- ¾ cup desiccated coconut
- Cooking spray
- 1 pound chicken breasts, skinless, boneless, and cubed

1. In a bowl, mix the desiccated coconut with garlic powder.
2. In another bowl, beat the eggs and season with salt and pepper.
3. Dip the chicken cubes in the egg mixture and then in the coconut mixture, making sure to coat them evenly.
4. Place the coated chicken in the air fryer basket and spray with cooking spray.
5. Cook at 180°C (or 360°F) for 20 minutes or until golden brown and crispy.
6. Serve as an appetizer or as a main dish with a side salad.

Charred Shishito Peppers

Prep time: 5 minutes | Cook time: 5 minutes | Serves 4

- 20 shishito peppers (about 170 grams)
- 1 teaspoon vegetable oil
- coarse sea salt
- 1 lemon

1. Preheat the air fryer to 200°C (392°F).
2. Toss the shishito peppers with the oil and salt. You can do this in a bowl or directly in the air fryer basket.
3. Air-fry at 200°C (392°F) for 5 minutes, shaking the basket once or twice while they cook.
4. Turn the charred peppers out into a bowl. Squeeze some lemon juice over the top and season with coarse sea salt. These should be served as finger foods – pick the pepper up by the stem and eat the whole pepper, seeds and all. Watch for that surprise spicy one!

Crispy Spiced Chickpeas

Prep time: 5 minutes | Cook time: 15 to 20 minutes | Serves 2 to 4

- 1 (400g) can chickpeas
- drained (or 1½ cups cooked chickpeas)
- ½ teaspoon salt
- ½ teaspoon chili powder
- ¼ teaspoon ground cinnamon
- ⅛ teaspoon smoked paprika
- pinch ground cayenne pepper
- 1 tablespoon olive oil

1. Pre-heat the air fryer to 200°C.
2. Dry the chickpeas as well as you can with a clean kitchen towel, rubbing off any loose skins as necessary. Combine the spices in a small bowl. Toss the chickpeas with the olive oil and then add the spices and toss again.
3. Air-fry for 15 minutes, shaking the basket a couple of times while they cook.
4. Check the chickpeas to see if they are crispy enough and if necessary, air-fry for another 5 minutes to crisp them further. Serve warm, or cool to room temperature and store in an airtight container for up to two weeks.

Buffalo Wings

Prep time: 5 minutes | Cook time: 22 minutes | Serves 2

- 1 kg chicken wings
- 3 tbsp butter, melted
- 60 ml hot sauce
- 1 tsp Worcestershire sauce
- Celery sticks, to serve
- Blue cheese dip, to serve

1. Preheat the oven to 200°C/180°C fan/gas mark 6.
2. Line a baking sheet with foil.
3. Cut off the chicken wing tips and discard them (or save for chicken stock). Cut through the joint to separate the drumettes and wingettes, and place them in a large bowl.
4. Combine the melted butter, hot sauce, and Worcestershire sauce in a small bowl. Pour the mixture over the chicken wings and toss to coat evenly.
5. Arrange the wings on the prepared baking sheet, and bake for 35-40 minutes or until cooked through and golden brown, turning once halfway through.
6. While the wings are cooking, mix together the remaining melted butter, hot sauce, and Worcestershire sauce in a small bowl.
7. When the wings are done, toss them in the finishing sauce to coat, and serve with celery sticks and blue cheese dip.

Goat Cheese Cauliflower and Bacon

Prep time: 5 minutes | Cook time: 20 minutes | Serves 4

- 8 cups cauliflower florets, roughly chopped
- 4 rashers of bacon, chopped
- Salt and black pepper to taste
- ½ cup spring onions, chopped
- 1 tablespoon garlic, minced
- 10 ounces goat cheese, crumbled
- ¼ cup soft cream cheese Cooking spray

1. Grease a baking dish that fits in the air fryer with cooking spray and mix all the ingredients except the goat cheese in the dish.
2. Sprinkle the goat cheese on top, put the dish in the air fryer, and cook at 200°C (400°F) for 20 minutes.
3. Divide the dish between plates and serve as a side dish.

Almond Broccoli Rice

Prep time: 10 minutes | Cook time: 8 minutes | Serves 4

- 2 cups broccoli, shredded
- ½ teaspoon apple cider vinegar
- ¼ teaspoon salt
- 1 tablespoon cream cheese
- ½ teaspoon pumpkin seeds, crushed
- 1 tablespoon organic almond milk
- 1 teaspoon butter, melted

1. In a bowl, mix together the melted butter, broccoli, apple cider vinegar, salt, and pumpkin seeds.
2. Transfer the mixture to a baking dish that fits in the air fryer.
3. Add the almond milk and mix the vegetables until well combined.
4. Cover the dish with foil.
5. Preheat the air fryer to 190°C (375°F).
6. Place the dish in the preheated air fryer and cook for 8 minutes.
7. Remove the dish from the air fryer and add the cream cheese.
8. Stir the cooked broccoli rice until well combined.

Chapter 5
Poultry Recipes

Kebab Skewers with Chicken & Tzatziki

Prep time: 5 minutes | Cooking time: 15 minutes | Serves 4

- 500 g chicken meat, preferably thighs
- 200 g zucchini
- 200 g cherry tomatoes
- 150 g paprika
- 1 onion
- 2 tbsp olive oil
- 3 tsp kebab seasoning
- 250 g Greek yogurt
- 100 g cucumber
- 2 tbsp olive oil
- 3 cloves of garlic
- sea salt
- pepper

1. Wash meat and pat dry Cut meat into pieces Wash and slice zucchini Wash and halve tomatoes Peel the onion and cut into pieces, then separate each layer.
2. Stir meat and vegetables alternately on wooden skewers Mix the olive oil, kebab seasoning and a little salt and pepper in a small bowl and brush the skewers all around with it.
3. Heat the air fryer and grill the skewers on all sides.
4. While doing so, wash and dry the cucumber, then finely grate with the grater Peel garlic cloves and press into a bowl
5. Add yogurt, cucumber and olive oil and season the Tzatziki with salt and pepper.

Chicken and Rice Casserole

Prep time: 5 minutes | Cook time: 35 minutes | Serves 4

- 2 cups cauliflower florets, chopped
- A pinch of salt and black pepper
- A drizzle of olive oil
- 6 ounces coconut cream
- 2 tablespoons butter, melted
- 2 teaspoons thyme, chopped
- 1 garlic clove, minced
- 1 tablespoon parsley, chopped
- 4 chicken thighs, boneless and skinless

1. Heat up a pan with the butter over medium heat, add the coconut cream and the other ingredients except the cauliflower, oil and the chicken, whisk, bring to a simmer and cook for 5 minutes.
2. Heat up a pan with the oil over medium-high heat, add the chicken and brown for 2 minutes on each side.
3. In a baking dish that fits the air fryer, mix the chicken with the cauliflower, spread the coconut cream mix all over, put the pan in the machine and cook at 190C/375F for 20 minutes.
4. Divide between plates and serve hot.

Chicken Wings and Vinegar Sauce

Prep time: 10 minutes | Cook time: 12 minutes | Serves 4

- 4 chicken wings
- 1 teaspoon Erythritol
- 1 teaspoon water
- 1 teaspoon apple cider vinegar
- 1 teaspoon salt
- ¼ teaspoon ground paprika
- ½ teaspoon dried oregano
- Cooking spray

1. Sprinkle the chicken wings with salt and dried oregano.
2. Then preheat the air fryer to 200C/180C fan/gas 6.
3. Place the chicken wings in the air fryer basket and cook them for 8 minutes.
4. Flip the chicken wings on another side after 4 minutes of cooking.
5. Meanwhile, mix up Erythritol, water, apple cider vinegar, and ground paprika in the saucepan and bring the liquid to boil.
6. Stir the liquid well and cook it until Erythritol is dissolved.
7. After this, generously brush the chicken wings with sweet Erythritol liquid and cook them in the air fryer at 200C/180C fan/gas 6 for 4 minutes more.

Gai Yang Chicken

Prep time: 10 minutes | Cook time: 65 minutes | Serves 4

- 2 pounds Cornish hens, roughly chopped
- 2 tablespoons Gai yang spices
- 1 tablespoon rapeseed oil

1. Rub the hens with spices carefully.
2. Then sprinkle the hens with rapeseed oil and put in the air fryer.
3. Cook the meal at 190C/375F for 65 minutes.

Smoked Paprika Chicken

Prep time: 10 minutes | Cook time: 20 minutes | Serves 4

- 2 pounds chicken breast, skinless, boneless
- 1 tablespoon smoked paprika
- 1 teaspoon coconut oil, melted
- 1 tablespoon cider vinegar

1. In a shallow bowl, mix the melted coconut oil, cider vinegar, and smoked paprika.
2. Brush the chicken breasts with the smoked paprika mixture.
3. Preheat the air fryer to 190°C (375°F).
4. Place the chicken in the air fryer basket and cook for 20 minutes, flipping the chicken halfway through the cooking time.
5. Serve hot.

Asian Chicken Salad

Prep time: 5 minutes | Cooking time: 20 minutes | Serves 4

- 300 g chicken meat
- 40 g rice noodles
- 1 carrot
- 100 g cucumber
- 1 red pepper
- ½ red onion
- 1 lime
- 1 clove of garlic
- 1 green chili pepper
- 2 tbsp cashew kernels or peanuts
- 2 sprigs of lemon basil or basil
- 200 ml vegetable broth
- 50 ml teriyaki sauce
- 2 tbsp of sesame oil
- Bamboo salt
- Pepper

1. Peel the carrot and cut into thin, short sticks. Wash the cucumber and cut into thin slices.
2. Cut the peppers in half and remove the kernels and partitions, then cut into thin strips.
3. Wash the lime hot and rub the skin, then halve the lime and squeeze out the juice.
4. Peel the onion and cut into tiny strips Peel and chop the garlic Halve the chili along and remove the seeds, then chop.
5. Wash the basil and shake dry, roughly chop the large leaves.
6. Heat the stock in a pot and heat the pasta in it. After the cooking time, drain the pasta and drain.
7. Place the carrot, cucumber, paprika, onion and noodles in a salad bowl, season with salt and pepper and mix.
8. Wash chicken meat and pat dry.
9. Heat the oil in an air fryer and fry the meat with garlic and chili all around golden brown. Add the teriyaki sauce, lime rub and some lime juice to the meat in the hot air fryer.
10. Turn the meat into it and allow to simmer briefly, then season with salt and pepper.
11. Pour noodles with vegetables in two bowls.
12. Add coarsely chopped nuts and basil Remove meat from the air fryer, cut into strips and serve warm on the salad.

Tomato Chicken Drumsticks

Prep time: 15 minutes + 8 hours for marinating | Cook time: 25 minutes | Serves 4

- 8 chicken drumsticks
- 15 ml tomato paste
- 5 ml cayenne pepper
- 30 ml apple cider vinegar
- 15 ml avocado oil

1. Mix tomato paste with cayenne pepper, apple cider vinegar, and avocado oil.
2. Then rub the chicken drumsticks with the tomato paste mixture and marinate for 8 hours.
3. Put the chicken drumsticks in the air fryer and cook at 180°C (356°F) for 18 minutes.

Coconut Turkey and Spinach Mix

Prep time: 5 minutes | Cook time: 15 minutes | Serves 4

- 450g turkey meat, ground and browned
- 1 tablespoon garlic, minced
- 1 tablespoon ginger, grated
- 2 tablespoons coconut aminos
- 120g spinach leaves
- A pinch of salt and black pepper

1. In a pan that fits your air fryer, combine the ground turkey, minced garlic, grated ginger, coconut aminos, spinach leaves, salt, and black pepper. Toss to coat everything evenly.
2. Put the pan in the air fryer and cook at 190 degrees Celsius (375 degrees Fahrenheit) for 15 minutes.
3. Divide everything into bowls and serve.

Keto Chicken Cauliflower Casserole

Prep time: 5 minutes | Cooking time: 55 minutes | Serves 4

- 1000 g chicken thighs
- 1 1/2 tsp chili powder
- 2 tbsp olive oil
- 150 g cream cheese
- 120 g of cheddar grated
- 160 g tomatoes
- 20 g Parmesan
- 40 g fresh cream
- 550 g cauliflower
- 30 g jalapeño
- salt
- pepper

1. Preheat the air fryer to 200° C (recirculation setting).
2. Cook the chicken for about 30 minutes and remove the meat from the bones.
3. Then fry the meat in a roasting air fryer until it turns brownish.
4. Add cream cheese and cheddar and stir.
5. Cut tomatoes into small pieces, add to them.
6. Mix everything well, season to taste with salt and pepper and then set aside.
7. Chop the cauliflower and jalapeño into small pieces.
8. Add the cauliflower, fresh cream and jalapeño over the meat and cheese mixture.
9. Sprinkle Parmesan over it, put it in the air fryer and bake for 20 minutes.

Cinnamon Chicken Wings

Prep time: 5 minutes | Cook time: 30 minutes | Serves 4

- 1 tablespoon olive oil
- 2 pounds of chicken wings
- 1 teaspoon ground cinnamon
- ½ teaspoon apple cider vinegar

1. Sprinkle the chicken wings with ground cinnamon and apple cider vinegar.
2. Then sprinkle the chicken wings with olive oil and put them in the air fryer.
3. Cook the wings at 190°C/375°F for 30 minutes, flipping them occasionally to ensure they cook evenly.

Chicken Cauliflower Casserole with Pesto

Prep time: 10 minutes | Cooking time: 40 minutes | Serves 6

- 244 g chicken thighs without skin
- 112 g of cheddar
- 120 g cream
- 140 g cauliflower
- 45 g leek
- 56 g tomato
- 28 g unsalted butter
- 16 g of keto pesto
- 1 tsp salt
- 1/2 tsp pepper

1. Preheat the air fryer to 180° C.
2. Heat butter in an air fryer.
3. Cut the chicken into pieces. Cook the chicken in the air fryer for about 6-8 minutes until golden brown.
4. Add salt and pepper to the chicken.
5. Mix pesto and cream.
6. Put the chicken in a casserole dish and add the pesto cream to the cream.
7. Chop cauliflower, tomato and leek into pieces.
8. Put the pieces of vegetables in the casserole dish.
9. Cut the cheese into small pieces and sprinkle on top.
10. Bake the casserole for 25-30 minutes.

Ginger Turkey and Cherry Tomatoes

Prep time: 5 minutes | Cook time: 25 minutes | Serves 4

- 1 pound turkey breast, skinless, boneless and cubed
- 240 ml double cream A pinch of salt and black pepper
- 113 g cherry tomatoes, halved
- 1 tablespoon ginger, grated
- 2 tablespoons red chilli powder
- 2 teaspoons olive oil

1. Heat up a pan that fits the air fryer with the oil over medium heat, add the turkey and brown for 2 minutes on each side.
2. Add the rest of the ingredients, toss, put the pan in the machine and cook at 190 degrees C for 20 minutes.
3. Divide everything between plates and serve.

Low-carb Pesto Chicken Roulade

Prep time: 10 minutes | Cooking time: 25 minutes | Serves 6

- 500 g chicken breast fillet 4 pieces
- 150 g halloumi-grilled cheese
- 250 ml Keto Pesto
- 1 tbsp olive oil
- 5 g a lemon peel
- 1 tsp garlic
- 1 tsp salt
- 1 tsp pepper
- 2 tbsp of olive oil for frying

1. Wash the chicken breast under running water. Dry well with paper towels.
2. Fillet the chicken breast as thinly as possible.
3. Knock the chicken breast fillets flat with a meat mallet (flat side).
4. Mix 250ml pesto (1/4 cup) with 1 tbsp of olive oil.
5. Distribute your pesto on the chicken breast.
6. Grate a bowl of 1 lemon over the chicken.
7. Cut the Halloumi cheese into small pieces and spread the cheese on the chicken.
8. Roll the fillets together as much as possible and fix them with chopsticks (maybe a toothpick).
9. Preheat the air fryer to 230 C.
10. Take a cast iron skillet (roast casserole too) and sprinkle with 2 tbsp olive oil.
11. Now fry the roulades in the air fryer, so that all sides are a little brown.
12. Then put everything in the air fryer and let it cook for 6-7 minutes.
13. Once clear juices run out of the roulade, remove from the air fryer, let rest briefly for 5-6 minutes and serve.

Philly Chicken Cheesesteak Stromboli

Prep time: 5 minutes | Cook time: 28 minutes | Serves 2 to 4

- ½ onion, sliced
- 1 teaspoon vegetable oil
- 2 boneless, skinless chicken breasts, partially frozen and sliced very thin on the bias (about 450g)
- 1 tablespoon Worcestershire sauce
- salt and freshly ground black pepper
- ½ recipe of Blue Jean Chef pizza dough, or 400g of store-bought pizza dough
- 170g grated Cheddar cheese
- 120g Cheese Whiz® (or other jarred cheese sauce), warmed gently in the microwave
- tomato ketchup for serving

1. Pre-heat the air fryer to 200°C.
2. Toss the sliced onion with oil and air-fry for 8 minutes, stirring halfway through the cooking time. Add the sliced chicken and Worcestershire sauce to the air fryer basket, and toss to evenly distribute the ingredients. Season the mixture with salt and freshly ground black pepper and air-fry for 8 minutes, stirring a couple of times during the cooking process. Remove the chicken and onion from the air fryer and let the mixture cool a little.
3. On a lightly floured surface, roll or press the pizza dough out into a 33cm by 28cm rectangle, with the long side closest to you. Sprinkle half of the Cheddar cheese over the dough leaving an empty 2.5cm border from the edge farthest away from you. Top the cheese with the chicken and onion mixture, spreading it out evenly. Drizzle the cheese sauce over the meat and sprinkle the remaining Cheddar cheese on top.
4. Start rolling the stromboli away from you and toward the empty border. Make sure the filling stays tightly tucked inside the roll. Finally, tuck the ends of the dough in and pinch the seam shut. Place the seam side down and shape the Stromboli into a U-shape to fit in the air-fry basket. Cut 4 small slits with the tip of a sharp knife evenly in the top of the dough and lightly brush the stromboli with a little oil.
5. Pre-heat the air fryer to 190°C.
6. Spray or brush the air fryer basket with oil and transfer the U-shaped stromboli to the air fryer basket. Air-fry for 12 minutes, turning the stromboli over halfway through the cooking time. (Use a plate to invert the stromboli out of the air fryer basket and then slide it back into the basket off the plate.)
7. To remove, carefully flip stromboli over onto a cutting board. Let it rest for a couple of minutes before serving. Slice the stromboli into 7.5cm pieces and serve with ketchup for dipping, if desired.

Tortilla Crusted Chicken Breast

Prep time: 5 minutes | Cook time: 12 minutes | Serves 2

- 80g flour
- 1 teaspoon salt
- 1½ teaspoons chili powder
- 1 teaspoon ground cumin
- freshly ground black pepper
- 1 egg, beaten
- 75g coarsely crushed yellow corn tortilla chips
- 2 (85-113g) boneless chicken breasts
- vegetable oil
- 125ml salsa
- 60g crumbled queso fresco
- fresh cilantro leaves
- sour cream or guacamole (optional)

1. Set up a dredging station with three shallow dishes. Combine the flour, salt, chili powder, cumin and black pepper in the first shallow dish. Beat the egg in the second shallow dish. Place the crushed tortilla chips in the third shallow dish.
2. Dredge the chicken in the spiced flour, covering all sides of the breast. Then dip the chicken into the egg, coating the chicken completely. Finally, place the chicken into the tortilla chips and press the chips onto the chicken to make sure they adhere to all sides of the breast. Spray the coated chicken breasts on both sides with vegetable oil.
3. Preheat the air fryer to 190°C.
4. Air-fry the chicken for 6 minutes. Then turn the chicken breasts over and air-fry for another 6 minutes. (Increase the cooking time if you are using chicken breasts larger than 85-113g.)
5. Let the chicken rest for a couple of minutes before slicing. Serve with salsa, queso fresco, cilantro leaves, and sour cream or guacamole, if desired.

Stuffed Chicken Breast Fillet

Prep time: 5 minutes | Cooking time: 50 minutes | Serves 4

- 600 g chicken breast fillet
- 120 g mozzarella
- 80 g of cheddar grated
- 1 tomato
- 30 g Keto Pesto
- salt
- pepper

1. Heat the air fryer to 180° C (convection).
2. Brush a casserole dish with oil, clean the meat with water and then dab it dry.
3. Slice the tomato and mozzarella cheese.
4. Cut the poultry meat transversely every 2 cm (do not cut through).
5. Alternating, place mozzarella and tomato slices in the cuts.
6. Season with pepper, place in a baking dish and sprinkle Cheddar over it.
7. Bake for 40 minutes and serve.

Chicken Thighs with Vegetables

Prep time: 10 minutes | Cooking time: 55 minutes | Serves 6

- 4 chicken legs, ready to cook
- 100 g cherry tomatoes
- 60 g mushrooms or other mushrooms
- 1 onion
- 6 tbsp olive oil
- 4 cloves of garlic
- 2 stalks of rosemary
- paprika
- sea salt
- pepper

1. Wash the chicken drumsticks and pat dry Peel the onion and cut into rings Wash the rosemary and shake it dry Crush the garlic cloves with the flat side of the knife.
2. Rub the chicken drumsticks all over with olive oil, paprika, salt, and pepper. Then place the thighs together with onion and garlic in a fireproof mold and place the rosemary on them. Boil thighs in a preheated air fryer at 200° C for 30 minutes.
3. While doing so, wash and halve the tomatoes Clean and slice the mushrooms Add both after 30 minutes to the thighs and cook everything for another 10-15 minutes until the thighs are cooked.

Chicken Cordon Bleu

Prep time: 8 minutes | Cooking time: 40 minutes | Serves 6

- 4 chicken fillets (150 g)
- 170 ml whipped cream
- 70 ml dry white wine
- 40 g butter
- 4 slices of Swiss cheese
- 4 slices of ham
- 15 g flour
- 2 tsp corn flour
- 3/4 block of chicken stock
- 3/4 tsp paprika powder
- salt and pepper to taste

1. Place the chicken fillets on a clean surface and smash them with a meat hammer. Place the ham and cheese slices on the chicken fillets and roll the chicken fillets. Secure the chicken fillets well with skewers.
2. Mix the flour, paprika, salt and pepper in a bowl. Sprinkle the chicken fillets with the flour and paprika powder mixture.
3. Heat the butter in an air fryer over medium heat and fry the chicken fillets until brown on all sides. Add the wine and chicken stock. Reduce the heat to low and cover the air fryer and let it cook for about 15 to 30 minutes, until the chicken is no longer pink on the inside.
4. Remove the skewers and place the chicken fillets on a warm dish. Mix the corn flour with the whipped cream in a small bowl and beat slowly in the frying air fryer. Cook this and keep stirring until the sauce is thick. Pour the sauce over the chicken fillets and serve.

Beef Steak with Broccoli

Prep time: 5 minutes | Cooking time: 25 minutes | Serves 4

- 120 g beef fillet or steak
- 60 g broccoli
- 30 g paprika
- ½ red onion
- 2 cloves of garlic
- 1 stalk of basil
- 1 sprig rosemary
- 2 tbsp olive oil
- sea salt
- pepper

1. Wash the peppers and cut into strips Peel the onion and cut into rings Peel and finely chop the garlic Wash the herbs and shake dry, peel the leaves from the basil and chop.
2. Wash the broccoli and cut the florets from the stalk Add the broccoli to a pot of water and steam, bring the water to a boil and cook the vegetables with the lid closed for 5 to 8 minutes.
3. Wash beef fillet and pat dry Heat the olive oil in the air fryer and add the fillet with rosemary together Fry the fillet for 3-5 minutes, depending on the thickness and desired cooking point, then remove, salt and pepper and let rest briefly.
4. Meanwhile, add the peppers, onion, and garlic to the hot air fryer and sauté. Season with salt and pepper.
5. Arrange broccoli, pate, and beef fillet on a plate. Pour basil over the meat and serve.

Chicken Breast with Arugula & Tomatoes

Prep time: 5 minutes | Cooking time: 20 minutes | Serves 4

- 140 g chicken breast fillet
- 50 g tomatoes
- 30 g arugula
- 10 g pine nuts
- 3 tbsp olive oil
- sea salt
- pepper

1. Wash the arugula and drain well, then remove long stalks.
2. Wash and quarter the tomatoes Brown the pine nuts in an air fryer without oil until golden brown, then remove and set aside Arrange the arugula, tomatoes and pine nuts on a plate and drizzle with 1 tbsp of olive oil.
3. Wash chicken breast and dab dry Heat 2 tbsp of olive oil in the air fryer and roast the meat on each side for about 6 to 10 minutes.
4. Remove the chicken breast from the air fryer, cut into strips and season with salt and pepper.

Chicken Breast with Air Fryer Vegetables

Prep time: 5 minutes | Cooking time: 25 minutes | Serves 4

- 180 g chicken breast, without skin
- 80 g Brussels sprouts
- 120 g carrot, fresh
- 120 g onion
- 1 pinch of sea salt
- 1 pinch of pepper, black
- 1 tbsp olive oil
- 1 stalk of parsley, fresh

1. Wash chicken breast and pat dry.
2. Remove the dry stem and withered leaves from the sprouts, then halve each time.
3. Peel carrot and slice. Peel the onion and cut into pieces. Wash the parsley and shake dry, then chop.
4. Heat the olive oil in the air fryer and fry the chicken breast on both sides until golden brown until the meat is cooked. Season the chicken breast with salt and pepper.
5. Add the vegetables to the hot air fryer and fry, then season with salt and pepper.

Chicken Breast with Peppered Vegetables

Prep time: 5 minutes | Cooking time: 25 minutes | Serves 4

- 1 chicken breast, without skin
- 50 g paprika, red, raw
- 50 g paprika, green, raw
- 50 g paprika, yellow, raw
- 1 onion, red
- 4 stems of coriander, fresh
- 1 pinch of sea salt
- 1 pinch of pepper, black
- 1 tbsp olive oil

1. Wash the chicken breast and dab it dry. Remove chili from cores and partitions and cut into strips. Peel onion and cut into rings. Wash the coriander and shake dry.
2. Heat the olive oil in the air fryer and fry the chicken breast on both sides until golden brown- the roasted chicken breast is served in a grill air fryer. Season the meat with salt and pepper, then remove from the air fryer.
3. Add the pepper strips and onions to the hot air fryer and fry briefly. Season the vegetables with salt and pepper.
4. Cut the chicken breast into strips and serve with the vegetables on a plate.

Chicken Breast with Green Beans

Prep time: 5 minutes | Cooking time: 20 minutes | Serves 4

- 1 chicken breast fillet, approx. 200 g
- 200 g green beans
- 2 tbsp olive oil
- 1 organic lemon
- sea salt
- pepper

1. Clean the beans and cook in an air fryer with water. Cook for 8-10 minutes. Wash and dry the chicken breast fillet. Brush the grill air fryer with oil and fry the meat on each side for 3 to 5 minutes, depending on the consistency of the meat.
2. Wash the lemon hot and dry, then rub the bowl with the grater.
3. Drain the beans and season with salt, pepper and lemon.
4. Halve the grated lemon in half and add some juice over the beans.
5. Season the fried chicken breast with salt and pepper and cut into strips Add the beans to the meat and serve everything together.

Chapter 6
Meat Recipes

Pork and Peppers Mix

Prep time: 5 minutes | Cook time: 25 minutes | Serves 4

- 1 pound pork tenderloin, sliced
- 25g fresh coriander, chopped
- ½ teaspoon garlic powder
- 1 tablespoon olive oil
- 1 green bell pepper, sliced into thin strips
- ½ teaspoon chili powder
- ½ teaspoon ground cumin

1. Heat a large frying pan with the oil over medium heat, add the pork and brown for 5 minutes.
2. Add the rest of the ingredients, toss together, and cook over medium heat for 20 minutes, stirring occasionally.
3. Once the pork is cooked through and the peppers are soft, divide the mixture between plates and serve.

Hot Pork Belly

Prep time: 15 minutes | Cook time: 40 minutes | Serves 6

- 1-pound pork belly
- 1 teaspoon ground black pepper
- 1 teaspoon salt
- 1 garlic clove, peeled, chopped
- 1 teaspoon chili powder
- 1 teaspoon dried chili flakes
- 1 teaspoon dried rosemary
- 1 tablespoon melted butter

1. Preheat your oven to 200°C/180°C Fan/Gas Mark 6.
2. Use a sharp knife to score the skin of the pork belly, making shallow cuts about 1cm apart.
3. Mix together the ground black pepper, salt, chili powder, chili flakes, and dried rosemary in a small bowl.
4. Rub the spice mixture all over the pork belly, making sure to get it into the cuts.
5. Fill the cuts with chopped garlic.
6. Brush the pork belly with melted butter.
7. Place the pork belly in a roasting tin and roast in the oven for 40 minutes, or until the pork is cooked through and the skin is crispy.
8. Once cooked, remove from the oven and let it rest for a few minutes before slicing and serving.

Dill Beef and Artichokes

Prep time: 5 minutes | Cook time: 30 minutes | Serves 4

- 1 and ½ pounds stewing beef, cubed
- A pinch of salt and black pepper
- 2 tablespoons olive oil
- 2 shallots, chopped
- 1 cup beef stock
- 2 garlic cloves, minced
- ½ teaspoon fresh dill, chopped
- 12 ounces canned artichoke hearts, drained and chopped

1. Heat a large frying pan with the oil over medium-high heat, add the beef and brown for 5 minutes.
2. Add the shallots, beef stock, minced garlic, and chopped artichoke hearts to the pan. Bring to a boil, then reduce the heat to low, cover the pan with a lid, and let simmer for 25 minutes.
3. Preheat the air fryer to 380°F/190°C.
4. Transfer the beef and artichoke mixture to an oven-safe dish and place it in the air fryer. Cook for an additional 5 minutes or until heated through.
5. Sprinkle the chopped dill over the top of the beef and artichoke mixture, then serve in bowls.

Lamb with Paprika Cilantro Sauce

Prep time: 5 minutes | Cook time: 30 minutes | Serves 4

- 1 pound lamb, cubed
- 1 cup coconut cream
- 3 tablespoons sweet paprika
- 2 tablespoons olive oil
- 2 tablespoons fresh coriander (cilantro), chopped
- Salt and black pepper to taste

1. Heat a large frying pan with the oil over medium-high heat, add the lamb and brown for 5 minutes.
2. Add the sweet paprika, coconut cream, salt, and black pepper to the pan. Stir to combine, then transfer the mixture to an oven-safe dish and place it in the air fryer.
3. Preheat the air fryer to 380°F/190°C and cook the lamb for 25 minutes.
4. Once the lamb is cooked, remove the dish from the air fryer and sprinkle chopped cilantro over the top.
5. Serve in bowls and enjoy your British Lamb with Paprika Cilantro Sauce!

Apple Cornbread Stuffed Pork Loin

Prep time: 10 minutes | Cook time: 61 minutes | Serves 4 to 6

- 4 rashers of streaky bacon, chopped
- 1 Granny Smith apple, peeled, cored and finely chopped
- 2 teaspoons fresh thyme leaves
- ¼ cup chopped fresh parsley
- 2 cups cubed cornbread
- ½ cup chicken stock
- salt and freshly ground black pepper
- 1 (2-pound) boneless pork loin
- kitchen twine
- 2 tablespoons butter
- 1 shallot, minced
- 1 Granny Smith apple, peeled, cored and finely chopped
- 3 sprigs fresh thyme
- 2 tablespoons flour
- 1 cup chicken stock
- ½ cup apple cider
- salt and freshly ground black pepper, to taste

1. Preheat the oven to 200°C/180°C fan/gas mark 6.
2. Add the bacon to a large frying pan over medium heat and cook for 6 to 8 minutes until crispy. While the bacon is cooking, combine the apple, fresh thyme, parsley, and cornbread in a bowl and toss well. Moisten the mixture with the chicken stock and season to taste with salt and freshly ground black pepper. Add the cooked bacon to the mixture.
3. Butterfly the pork loin by holding it flat on the cutting board with one hand, while slicing into the pork loin parallel to the cutting board with the other. Slice into the longest side of the pork loin, but stop before you cut all the way through. You should then be able to open the pork loin up like a book, making it twice as wide as it was when you started. Season the inside of the pork with salt and freshly ground black pepper.
4. Spread the cornbread mixture onto the butterflied pork loin, leaving a one-inch border around the edge of the pork. Roll the pork loin up around the stuffing to enclose the stuffing, and tie the rolled pork in several places with kitchen twine or secure with toothpicks. Try to replace any stuffing that falls out of the roast as you roll it, by stuffing it into the ends of the rolled pork. Season the outside of the pork with salt and freshly ground black pepper.
5. Place the stuffed pork loin into a roasting tray, seam side down. Roast the pork loin for 15 minutes at 200°C/180°C fan/gas mark 6. Turn the pork loin over and roast for an additional 15 minutes. Turn the pork loin a quarter turn and roast for an additional 15 minutes. Turn the pork loin over again to expose the fourth side, and roast for an additional 10 minutes. The pork loin should register 155°F (68°C) on an instant-read thermometer when it is finished.
6. While the pork is cooking, make the apple gravy. Preheat a saucepan over medium heat on the stovetop and melt the butter. Add the shallot, apple, and thyme sprigs and sauté until the apple starts to soften and brown a little. Add the flour and stir for a minute or two. Whisk in the stock and apple cider vigorously to prevent the flour from forming lumps. Bring the mixture to a boil to thicken and season to taste with salt and pepper.
7. Transfer the pork loin to a resting plate and loosely tent with foil, letting the pork rest for at least 5 minutes before slicing and serving with the apple gravy poured over the top.

Fresh Garden Salad with Beef

Prep time: 5 minutes | Cooking time: 15 minutes | Serves 4

- 180 g beef steak, organic
- 50 g mixed lettuce
- 5 cherry tomatoes
- 3 radishes
- 1 carrot
- 6 sprigs of thyme
- 1 sprig rosemary
- 3 tbsp olive oil
- sea salt
- pepper

1. Wash lettuce leaves and dry them in a salad spinner Pare large lettuce leaves Peel the carrot and cut into thin slices with Clean peeler radish and slice Wash tomatoes and cut in half.
2. Wash thyme and rosemary and shake dry Wash beef steak and dry with a kitchen crepe Heat 2 tbsp of oil in the air fryer
3. Add the herbs and steak and fry the meat on both sides for a short while.
4. Remove steak from the air fryer, season with salt and pepper and let it rest for a short while.
5. Place the prepared salad ingredients on a plate and season with salt and pepper.
6. Pour 1 tbsp of olive oil over the salad. Slice the steak and add to the salad.

Smoked Pork Chops with Pickled Cabbage

Prep time: 5 minutes | Cooking time: 20 minutes | Serves 4

- 150 g Kassel
- 150 g sauerkraut
- 1/4 onion
- 1 bay leaf
- Black peppercorns, optional
- 3 cloves, optional
- Juniper berries, optional

1. Moisten a coated air fryer with a little oil.
2. Roast Kassel on both sides until it turns a bit brownish on the outside.
3. Then season with pepper.
4. Drain the herbs and heat in an air fryer.

Cinnamon Lamb Meatloaf

Prep time: 5 minutes | Cook time: 35 minutes | Serves 4

- 2 pounds lamb, minced
- A pinch of salt and black pepper
- ½ teaspoon hot paprika
- A drizzle of olive oil
- 2 tablespoons parsley, chopped
- 2 tablespoons coriander, chopped
- 1 teaspoon ground cumin
- ¼ teaspoon ground cinnamon
- 1 teaspoon ground coriander
- 1 egg
- 2 tablespoons tomato ketchup
- 4 spring onions, chopped
- 1 teaspoon lemon juice

1. In a bowl, combine the lamb with the rest of the ingredients except the oil and mix well.
2. Grease a loaf tin that fits into the air fryer with the oil, add the lamb mixture and shape the meatloaf.
3. Place the tin in the air fryer and cook at 190°C (375°F) for 35 minutes.
4. Slice and serve.

Pork Schnitzel with Dill Sauce

Prep time: 10 minutes | Cook time: 24 minutes | Serves 4 to 6

- 6 boneless, center cut pork chops (about 1.5 pounds)
- 120g plain flour
- 1.5 teaspoons salt
- freshly ground black pepper
- 2 medium eggs
- 120ml milk
- 180g toasted fine breadcrumbs
- 1 teaspoon paprika
- 3 tablespoons butter, melted
- 2 tablespoons vegetable or olive oil
- lemon wedges
- 240ml chicken stock
- 1.5 tablespoons cornflour
- 80ml sour cream
- 1.5 tablespoons chopped fresh dill
- salt and pepper

1. Trim the excess fat from the pork chops and pound each chop with a meat mallet between two pieces of cling film until they are 1.25 cm thick.
2. Set up a dredging station. Combine the flour, salt, and black pepper in a shallow dish. Whisk the eggs and milk together in a second shallow dish. Finally, combine the breadcrumbs and paprika in a third shallow dish.
3. Dip each flattened pork chop in the flour. Shake off the excess flour and dip each chop into the egg mixture. Finally, dip them into the breadcrumbs and press the breadcrumbs onto the meat firmly. Place each finished chop on a baking sheet until they are all coated.
4. Preheat the air fryer to 200°C.
5. Combine the melted butter and the oil in a small bowl and lightly brush both sides of the coated pork chops. Do not brush the chops too heavily or the breading will not be as crispy.
6. Air-fry one schnitzel at a time for 4 minutes, turning it over halfway through the cooking time. Hold the cooked schnitzels warm on a baking pan in a 80°C oven while you finish air-frying the rest.
7. While the schnitzels are cooking, whisk the chicken stock and cornflour together in a small saucepan over medium-high heat on the stovetop. Bring the mixture to a boil and simmer for 2 minutes. Remove the saucepan from heat and whisk in the sour cream. Add the chopped fresh dill and season with salt and pepper.
8. Transfer the pork schnitzel to a platter and serve with dill sauce and lemon wedges. For a traditional meal, serve this alongside some egg noodles, spaetzle or German potato salad.

Spicy Lamb Sirloin Steak

Prep time: 15 minutes | Cooking time: 40 minutes | Serves 4

- 1 teaspoon ground fennel
- 1 teaspoon ground cinnamon
- 1/2 teaspoon ground cardamom
- 1/2 onion
- 4 slices ginger
- 1 teaspoon garam masala
- 1/2 - 1 teaspoon cayenne
- 1 teaspoon salt
- lamb sirloin steaks

1. In a food processor, combine all ingredients except for the lamb steaks and pulse until the mixture becomes a paste.
2. Spread the paste all over the lamb steaks and allow them to marinate for 30 minutes or up to 24 hours in the refrigerator.
3. Preheat your air fryer to 170°C (338°F) for 15 minutes.
4. Place the lamb steaks in a single layer in the air fryer basket and cook for 10 minutes on each side, flipping halfway through.
5. Check the internal temperature of the lamb with a meat thermometer and ensure it reaches at least 70°C (158°F) for medium-well.
6. Serve hot and enjoy!

Beef Pot Roast

Prep time: 10 minutes | Cooking time: 2 hours 20 minutes | Serves 8

- 800 g beef stew
- 150 ml red wine
- 3 garlic (toes)
- 1 tbsp tomato concentrate
- 400 ml beef stock
- 1-star anise
- 1 tsp Ras el hanout
- 2 bay leaves, dried
- 6 stems thyme, fresh
- 1 tsp of sea salt
- 1 tsp pepper, black
- 1 tbsp olive oil

1. Wash beef stew and pat dry, then chop into cubes. Wash thyme stalks and shake dry. Peel and crush the garlic with the flat side of the knife.
2. Heat the olive oil in the braised air fryer. Add the beef, garlic, and thyme to the air fryer and sauté the meat all around. Add the tomato puree and sauté.
3. Douse everything with red wine and cook it briefly. Fill up with cattle stock, then add sternalis, bay leaves, and a little salt and pepper. Simmer meat with lid closed for 10 minutes.
4. Place in the 160° C preheated air fryer and cook the beef for about 2 hours. After half of the cooking time, turn the pieces of beef or stir once.
5. Remove the finished beef stew from the air fryer and let it rest briefly. Add fresh herbs as desired and serve with a salad.

Creamy Pork Schnitzel

Prep time: 15 minutes | Cook time: 10 minutes | Serves 2

- 4 pork cutlets (2 oz each cutlet)
- 1 teaspoon sunflower oil
- 1 egg, beaten
- 1 tablespoon double cream
- ½ cup almond flour
- ½ teaspoon ground black pepper
- ½ teaspoon salt

1. Flatten the pork cutlets with a meat mallet and season with ground black pepper and salt.
2. In a bowl, mix the beaten egg and double cream.
3. Dip the pork cutlets in the egg mixture and then coat in the almond flour.
4. Repeat the same steps one more time.
5. Preheat the air fryer to 200°C (400°F).
6. Sprinkle the pork cutlets with sunflower oil and place them in the air fryer.
7. Cook the schnitzels for 5 minutes on each side.

Beef Steak with Arugula Cherry Tomatoes

Prep time: 5 minutes | Cooking time: 10 minutes | Serves 4

- 1 beef steak hip, sliced
- 100 g cherry tomatoes
- 20 g arugula, fresh
- 1 stalk of rosemary, fresh
- 1 pinch of sea salt
- 1 pinch of pepper, black
- 30 g butter
- 1 tbsp olive oil

1. Wash beef and pat dry. Wash rosemary and shake dry.
2. Heat the butter and oil in the air fryer, then add the beef steak with the sprig rosemary.
3. Fry the steak for a few minutes, then turn over and roast on the other side for a few minutes, depending on the desired cooking level. Season the steak with salt and pepper and serve on a plate.
4. Meanwhile, wash the arugula and dry in the salad spinner. Wash tomatoes and drain, then cut in half.
5. Add arugula and tomatoes to the steak and then season everything with salt and pepper.

Sweet Pork Belly

Prep time: 15 minutes | Cook time: 55 minutes | Serves 6

- 450g pork belly
- 1 teaspoon sweetener (such as Stevia)
- 1 teaspoon salt
- 1 teaspoon white pepper
- 1 teaspoon butter, softened
- 1/2 teaspoon onion powder

1. Sprinkle the pork belly with salt, white pepper, and onion powder.
2. Preheat the air fryer to 196°C / 385°F.
3. Place the pork belly in the air fryer and cook for 45 minutes.
4. Turn the pork belly over and spread with butter.
5. Sprinkle the sweetener on top of the pork belly and cook for another 10 minutes at 204°C / 400°F.

Beef, Lettuce and Cabbage Salad

Prep time: 5 minutes | Cook time: 25 minutes | Serves 4

- 450g beef, cubed
- 60ml coconut aminos
- 15ml coconut oil, melted
- 170g iceberg lettuce, shredded
- 30ml cilantro, chopped
- 30ml chives, chopped
- 1 courgette, shredded
- 1/2 small green cabbage head, shredded
- 30g almonds, sliced
- 15ml sesame seeds
- 7.5ml white vinegar
- A pinch of salt and black pepper

1. Heat up a pan over medium-high heat, add the oil and brown the beef for 5 minutes.
2. Add the aminos, zucchini, cabbage, salt, and pepper. Toss well, put the pan in the air fryer and cook at 190°C for 20 minutes.
3. Allow the mixture to cool down, transfer to a salad bowl, add the rest of the ingredients, and toss well before serving.

Fried Egg & Bacon

Prep time: 5 minutes | Cooking time: 15 minutes | Serves 4

- 2 eggs
- 30 g bacon
- 2 tbsp olive oil
- sea salt
- pepper

1. Heat the oil in the air fryer and fry the bacon slices. Then reduce the heat and add the eggs to the air fryer.
2. Fry the eggs over medium heat and season with salt and pepper.

Keto Pork Ribs

Prep time: 5 minutes | Cooking time: 2 hours 20 minutes | Serves 8

- Spareribs
- 1 kg ribs peeling rib of pork
- 360 ml chicken broth
- 45 ml lime juice
- 1 tsp garlic chopped
- 1 tsp salt
- Sauce
- 180 ml mayonnaise
- 45 ml lime juice
- 40 g shallots
- 10 g garlic
- 1 handful of parsley
- 1/2 tsp salt

SPARERIBS

1. Preheat the air fryer to 150° C.
2. Place ribs in the air fryer. Sprinkle with salt and add stock, lime juice and garlic.
3. Close tightly with a lid or aluminum foil and place in the air fryer for approx. 2 hours.

SAUCE

1. Peel shallots and garlic.
2. Place in a blender and add the remaining ingredients.
3. Puree and add to the ribs.

Keto Mini Burger

Prep time: 5 minutes | Cooking time: 20 minutes | Serves 4

- 400 g ground beef
- 50 ml coconut oil
- 1/2 tsp coriander ground
- Ground 1/2 tsp cumin
- 1/2 tsp cayenne pepper ground
- salt
- pepper
- Optional Toppings:
- 200 g tomato
- 150 g bacon
- 40 g onion
- 1 tbsp of parsley fresh
- 50 g mayonnaise bought or homemade

1. Mix the minced meat with the spices and make 12 small patties.
2. Heat the coconut oil in an air fryer and fry the patties well.
3. Peel the onion and cut it into rings. Wash and slice the tomato.
4. Cut the bacon into small pieces and sauté briefly in the air fryer.
5. Add a tsp of mayonnaise and top with tomato, onion, parsley and bacon.

Chapter 7
Fish and Seafood Recipes

Balsamic Cod

Prep time: 5 minutes | Cook time: 15 minutes | Serves 4

- 4 cod fillets, boneless
- Salt and black pepper to taste
- 1 cup parmesan
- 4 tablespoons balsamic vinegar
- A drizzle of olive oil
- 3 spring onions, chopped

1. Season the fish with salt and pepper, then brush with the olive oil and coat in parmesan.
2. Place the fillets in your air fryer's basket and cook at 190 degrees Celsius for 14 minutes.
3. In a bowl, mix the spring onions with salt, pepper and the vinegar and whisk.
4. Divide the cod between plates, drizzle the spring onion mixture over and serve with a side salad.

Salmon and Lime Sauce

Prep time: 5 minutes | Cook time: 20 minutes | Serves 4

- 4 salmon fillets, boneless
- 120ml coconut cream
- 1 teaspoon lime zest, grated
- 80ml double cream
- 60ml lime juice
- 50g desiccated coconut
- A pinch of salt and black pepper

1. In a bowl, mix all the ingredients except the salmon and whisk.
2. Arrange the fish in a dish that fits your air fryer, drizzle the coconut sauce all over, put the dish in the machine and cook at 180 degrees Celsius for 20 minutes.
3. Divide between plates and serve.

Lemon Prawn and Courgettes

Prep time: 5 minutes | Cook time: 15 minutes | Serves 4

- 1 pound prawns, peeled and deveined
- A pinch of salt and black pepper
- 2 courgettes, cut into medium cubes
- 1 tablespoon lemon juice
- 1 tablespoon olive oil
- 1 tablespoon garlic, minced

1. In a pan that fits the air fryer, combine all the ingredients, toss, put the pan in the machine and cook at 190 degrees Celsius (370 degrees F) for 15 minutes.
2. Divide between plates and serve immediately.

Parmesan and Garlic Trout

Prep time: 5 minutes | Cook time: 15 minutes | Serves 4

- 2 tablespoons olive oil
- 2 garlic cloves, minced
- 120ml chicken stock
- Salt and black pepper, to taste
- 4 trout fillets, boneless
- 75g Parmesan cheese, grated
- 15g tarragon, chopped

1. In a pan that fits your air fryer, mix the olive oil, garlic, chicken stock, salt and black pepper and whisk well.
2. Add the trout fillets and coat them well with the mixture.
3. Sprinkle the grated Parmesan cheese and chopped tarragon over the fillets.
4. Place the pan in the air fryer and cook at 190°C/375°F for 15 minutes.
5. Divide the trout fillets between plates and serve.

Shrimp Spiesse

Prep time: 5 minutes | Cooking time: 10 minutes | Serves 4

- 225 g of shrimp
- 1/2 tbsp of lemon juice
- salt
- pepper
- Chili flakes

1. Thaw shrimp and stick on 5 wooden skewers.
2. Fry in an air fryer coated with olive oil.
3. Drizzle with lemon juice.
4. Season to taste with salt, pepper and chili flakes.

Chili Squid Rings

Prep time:15 minutes |Cook time: 10 minutes |Serves 2

- 225g squid tube, trimmed, washed
- 115g chorizo, chopped
- 1 teaspoon olive oil
- 1 teaspoon chili flakes
- 1 tablespoon keto mayonnaise

1. Preheat the air fryer to 200C and put the chopped chorizo in the air fryer basket.
2. Sprinkle it with chili flakes and olive oil and cook for 6 minutes.
3. Then shake chorizo well.
4. Slice the squid tube into the rings and add in the air fryer.
5. Cook the meal for 4 minutes at 200C.
6. Shake the cooked meal well and transfer it to plates.
7. Sprinkle the meal with keto mayonnaise.

Trout with Herbs de Provance

Prep time: 10 minutes | Cook time: 20 minutes | Serves 4

- 2-pound trout fillet
- 1 tablespoon olive oil
- 1 tablespoon Herbs de Provence

1. Rub the trout with Herbs de Provence and sprinkle with olive oil.
2. Put the fish in the air fryer basket and cook at 190°C for 10 minutes per side.

Grilled Salmon with Green Beans

Prep time: 5 minutes | Cooking time: 20 minutes | Serves 4

- 1 salmon fillet, approx. 300 g
- 500 g green beans
- 2 tbsp butter
- 1 organic lemon
- 1 clove of garlic
- 4 sprigs of thyme
- 1 sprig rosemary
- 4 tbsp olive oil
- sea salt
- pepper

1. Wash the salmon fillet and pat dry Peel and finely chop the garlic Wash and dry the herbs, then pluck the leaves from the stalk and chop finely.
2. Mix the garlic, herbs and oil in a flat shape, then marinate the fish and leave to infuse.
3. Clean the beans and cook in a pot of water for about 8 minutes until they are cooked
4. Drain the beans and drain.
5. Cut the lemon into pieces.
6. Heat the grill air fryer and grill the salmon fillet until it has the roast strips, then turn and grill on the second side. The salmon fillet can also be prepared on the grill as desired.
7. In the meantime, melt the butter in a second air fryer and stir in the beans.
8. Then season the beans with a little lemon juice, salt and pepper and divide them into two plates.
9. Season the salmon fillet with salt and pepper. Halve the fillet piece and arrange half of each on the beans.
10. Add the lemon pieces, then sprinkle some lemon juice over the fish and serve.

Parmesan Mackerel

Prep time: 10 minutes | Cook time: 7 minutes | Serves 2

- 340g mackerel fillet
- 57g Parmesan, grated
- 1 teaspoon ground coriander
- 1 tablespoon olive oil

1. Brush the mackerel fillet with olive oil and place it in the air fryer basket.
2. Sprinkle the fillet with ground coriander and Parmesan cheese.
3. Cook the fish in the air fryer at 200°C for 7 minutes.

Salmon Cheese Air Fryer Cakes

Prep time: 5 minutes | Cooking time: 20 minutes | Serves 4

- 3 eggs
- 80 g cream cheese
- 40 g cream cheese
- 85 g smoked salmon

1. Mix the dough of cream cheese and eggs.
2. Bake air fryer cakes in air fryer.
3. Spread air fryer cakes with cream cheese, place the salmon on it and roll up the air fryer cakes.

Spicy Fish Street Tacos

Prep time: 10 minutes | Cook time: 5 minutes | Serves 2 to 3

FOR THE SRIRACHA SLAW:
- 120ml mayonnaise
- 2 tablespoons rice vinegar
- 1 teaspoon sugar
- 2 tablespoons sriracha chili sauce
- 5 cups shredded white cabbage
- 60g shredded carrots
- 2 scallions, chopped
- Salt and freshly ground black pepper

FOR THE FISH:
- 70g plain flour
- 1 teaspoon chili powder
- ½ teaspoon ground cumin
- 1 teaspoon salt
- Freshly ground black pepper
- ½ teaspoon baking powder
- 1 egg, beaten
- 60ml milk
- 100g breadcrumbs
- 450g mahi-mahi or snapper fillets, cut into 1-inch wide sticks, approximately 4-inches long
- 1 tablespoon canola or vegetable oil
- 6 (6-inch) flour tortillas
- 1 lime, cut into wedges

1. Start by making the sriracha slaw. Combine the mayonnaise, rice vinegar, sugar, and sriracha sauce in a large bowl. Mix well and add the white cabbage, carrots, and scallions. Toss until all the vegetables are coated with the dressing and season with salt and pepper. Refrigerate the slaw until you are ready to serve the tacos.
2. Combine the flour, chili powder, cumin, salt, pepper, and baking powder in a bowl. Add the egg and milk and mix until the batter is smooth. Place the breadcrumbs in shallow dish.
3. Dip the fish sticks into the batter, coating all sides. Let the excess batter drip off the fish and then roll them in the breadcrumbs, patting the crumbs onto all sides of the fish sticks. Set the coated fish on a plate or baking sheet until all the fish has been coated.
4. Preheat the air fryer to 200°C/400°F.
5. Spray the coated fish sticks with oil on all sides. Spray or brush the inside of the air fryer basket with oil and transfer the fish to the basket. Place as many sticks as you can in one layer, leaving a little room around each stick. Place any remaining sticks on top, perpendicular to the first layer.
6. Air-fry the fish for 3 minutes. Turn the fish sticks over and air-fry for an additional 2 minutes.
7. While the fish is air-frying, warm the tortilla shells either in a 180°C/350°F oven wrapped in foil or in a skillet with a little oil over medium-high heat for a couple of minutes. Fold the tortillas in half and keep them warm until the remaining tortillas and fish are ready.
8. To assemble the tacos, place two pieces of the fish in each tortilla shell and top with the sriracha slaw. Squeeze the lime wedge over top and dig in.

Trout and Tomato Courgette Mix

Prep time: 5 minutes | Cook time: 15 minutes | Serves 4

- 3 zucchinis, cut in medium chunks
- 4 trout fillets, boneless
- 2 tablespoons olive oil
- 60ml keto tomato sauce
- Salt and black pepper to the taste
- 1 garlic clove, minced
- 1 tablespoon lemon juice
- 30g cilantro, chopped

1. In a pan that fits your air fryer, mix the fish with the other ingredients, toss, introduce in the fryer and cook at 193 degrees Celsius for 15 minutes.
2. Divide everything between plates and serve right away.

French Clams

Prep time: 5 minutes | Cook time: 3 minutes | Serves 5

- 2-pounds clams, raw, shells removed
- 1 tablespoon Herbs de Provence
- 1 tablespoon sesame oil
- 1 garlic clove, chopped

1. Put the clams in a bowl and sprinkle with Herbs de Provence, sesame oil, and chopped garlic.
2. Toss the clams well.
3. Preheat the air fryer to 200°C/180°C fan/gas 6.
4. Place the clams in the air fryer and cook for 3 minutes.
5. Once the clams are cooked, toss them again and transfer them to serving plates.

Salmon In Zucchini Bed

Prep time: 5 minutes | Cooking time: 30 minutes | Serves 4

- 250 g salmon fillet
- 1 lemon
- 1 zucchini
- 2 tomatoes
- 30 g onion red
- 1 tbsp olive oil
- 1 clove of garlic
- Dressed thyme
- Dill, dried
- Fresh rosemary
- salt
- pepper

1. Preheat air fryer to 150° C convection.
2. Line 2 bowls with aluminum foil.
3. Slice the zucchini and lemon and spread in the bowls.
4. Put the salmon in the aluminum bowls and top with pieces of tomato.
5. Chop the onion and garlic.
6. Distribute all ingredients on the salmon.
7. Season with salt and pepper.
8. Put herbs in the bowls and close aluminum foil well.
9. Bake in the air fryer for 20 minutes.

Zoodles with Shrimp & Cherry Tomatoes

Prep time: 5 minutes | Cooking time: 20 minutes | Serves 4

- 500 g zucchini
- 200 g shrimp, without the head, with shell
- 200 g cherry tomatoes
- 2 shallots
- 2 cloves of garlic
- 1 organic lemon
- 200 ml vegetable broth
- 50 ml sesame oil
- sea salt
- pepper

1. Wash and dry the zucchini Cut into long thin noodles with the spiral cutter Wash the tomatoes and drain them, then quarter them Peel the shallots and finely dice Peel the garlic and finely chop.
2. Wash the lemon hot and dry, then grate the skin with the grater then halve the lemon and squeeze out the juice Remove shrimp from the shell, do not throw the bowl aside, but set aside for frying-this gives a great flavor.
3. Heat the sesame oil in the air fryer and fry the garlic, shallots, shrimp and shrimp shells. Add the tomatoes and stir everything. Remove the shrimp and set aside. Take out the shrimp shells as well. These can now be disposed of.
4. Put the zucchini noodles in the hot air fryer and fill with stock. Sauté the zucchini noodles for 3-4 minutes. Add the grated lemon peel and a little lemon juice and season with salt and pepper.
5. Stir everything again, then add the shrimp again and briefly warm.

Tuna with Vegetables & Avocado

Prep time: 5 minutes | Cooking time: 15 minutes | Serves 4

- 150 g tuna, canned
- 1 avocado
- 100 g paprika
- 100 g tomatoes
- 50 g cucumber
- 1 spring onion
- 30 g corn, from the tin
- ½ bunch of parsley
- 50 g radish
- ½ chili pepper
- 1 lime
- 2 tbsp olive oil
- nutmeg
- sea salt
- pepper

1. Open the tuna can a piece and drain the juice, then open the tin completely and tuck the tuna into pieces with the fork Halve the avocado and remove the kernel Halve the lime and squeeze the juice Sprinkle both avocado halves with a little lime juice.
2. Peel the cucumber and then cut it into pieces. Remove the peppers from the seeds and partitions and cut into small cubes. Wash the tomatoes and cut into pieces. Clean the spring onion and cut into rings.
3. Pour corn into a sieve and drain Wash the parsley and shake it dry, then peel and chop the leaves Chop the chili lengthwise and core lengthwise, then chop finely Clean the radish and cut into small pieces.
4. Put the tuna, cucumber, peppers, tomatoes, spring onions, corn, parsley, radishes and chili pepper in a bowl. Add the olive oil and some lime juice and season with grated nutmeg, salt, and pepper. Mix the salad well, then serve together with the avocado.

Fried Crawfish

Prep time:10 minutes |Cook time: 5 minutes |Serves 4

- 450g crawfish
- 1 tablespoon rapeseed oil
- 1 teaspoon onion powder
- 1 tablespoon fresh rosemary, chopped

1. Preheat the air fryer to 170°C (340°F).
2. Place the crawfish in the air fryer basket and sprinkle with rapeseed oil and rosemary.
3. Add the onion powder and stir the crawfish gently to evenly coat.
4. Cook for 5 minutes until the crawfish are cooked through and crispy. Serve hot.

Mint Sardines

Prep time: 10 minutes | Cook time: 16 minutes |Serves 4

- 1 pound sardines, trimmed and cleaned
- 1 teaspoon dried mint
- 1 teaspoon olive oil
- 1/2 teaspoon salt
- 1/2 teaspoon ground black pepper

1. Preheat the air fryer to 190°C (375°F).
2. In a small bowl, mix together the dried mint, olive oil, salt, and ground black pepper.
3. Rub the mixture onto the sardines, making sure to coat both sides.
4. Place the sardines in the air fryer basket in a single layer.
5. Air fry for 8 minutes on one side, then flip the sardines over and air fry for an additional 8 minutes on the other side, or until fully cooked and crispy.
6. Serve hot.

Garlic Fish and Balsamic Salsa

Prep time: 5 minutes | Cook time: 15 minutes | Serves 4

- 4 sea bass fillets, boneless
- 1 tablespoon olive oil
- 3 tomatoes, roughly chopped
- 2 spring onions, chopped
- 60ml chicken stock (about 1/4 cup)
- A pinch of salt and black pepper
- 3 garlic cloves, minced
- 1 tablespoon balsamic vinegar

1. In a food processor or blender, combine all the ingredients except the fish and pulse until well blended.
2. Pour the mixture into a pan that fits the air fryer, add the fish, and toss gently to coat.
3. Place the pan into the air fryer and cook at 190°C (375°F) for 15 minutes.
4. Divide between plates and serve.

Tender Salmon

Prep time: 10 minutes | Cook time: 9 minutes | Serves 3

- 450g salmon
- 1 teaspoon dried rosemary
- 2 tablespoons olive oil
- ½ teaspoon salt

1. Sprinkle the salmon with dried rosemary, olive oil, and salt.
2. Put the salmon in the air fryer and cook at 200°C (or 180°C fan) for 9 minutes.

Roasted Tilapia

Prep time: 5 minutes | Cook time: 20 minutes | Serves 4

- 4 tilapia fillets, boneless and halved
- 1 tablespoon rapeseed oil
- 1 teaspoon ground turmeric

1. Sprinkle the tilapia fillets with rapeseed oil and ground turmeric.
2. Put them in the air fryer and cook at 185°C (365°F) for 10 minutes per side.

Lime Lobster Tail

Prep time: 10 minutes | Cook time: 6 minutes | Serves 4

- 4 lobster tails, peeled
- 2 tablespoons lime juice
- 1/2 teaspoon dried basil
- 1/2 teaspoon melted coconut oil

1. In a bowl, mix together the lobster tails, lime juice, dried basil, and melted coconut oil.
2. Place the lobster tails in the air fryer and cook at 190°C (375°F) for 6 minutes.

Salmon, Egg & Parmesan Salad

Prep time: 5 minutes | Cooking time: 20 minutes | Serves 4

- 200 g of salmon
- 4 eggs
- 200 g Romana salad
- 100 g arugula
- 10 cherry tomatoes
- 1 organic lemon
- 50 g Parmesan
- 5 tbsp olive oil
- Balsamic-Date & fig at the pleasure
- sea salt
- pepper

1. Cook the eggs in a pot of boiling water for 8-10 minutes. Then chill the eggs cold, peel and cut in half.
2. Wash lettuce leaves and dry in a salad spinner, then pluck small Wash tomatoes, drain and then halve
3. Place lettuce leaves and tomatoes on two plates and drizzle with 1 tbsp of oil.
4. Wash salmon and dab it dry. Cut the salmon into bite-sized pieces.
5. Heat 3 tbsp of oil in the air fryer and roast the salmon pieces all around. Season the salmon with salt and pepper and add to the salad.
6. Add the eggs to the salad and sprinkle with freshly grated Parmesan cheese
7. Halve the lemon and drizzle some juice over the salmon and salad.
8. Finally, refine the salad with balsamic.

Chapter 8
Vegetable Recipes

Mozzarella Asparagus Mix

Prep time: 5 minutes | Cook time: 10 minutes | Serves 4

- 450g asparagus, trimmed
- 2 tablespoons olive oil
- Pinch of salt and black pepper
- 200g mozzarella, shredded
- 120ml balsamic vinegar
- 400g cherry tomatoes, halved

1. In a pan that fits your air fryer, mix the asparagus with the rest of the ingredients except the mozzarella and toss.
2. Put the pan in the air fryer and cook at 200 degrees Celsius for 10 minutes.
3. Divide between plates and serve.

Cheesy Green Patties

Prep time: 20 minutes | Cook time: 6 minutes | Serves 2

- 225g fresh spinach, chopped
- 85g provolone cheese, shredded
- 1 egg, beaten
- 30g almond flour
- ½ teaspoon salt
- Cooking spray

1. Put the chopped spinach in the blender and blend it until you get a smooth mixture.
2. After this, transfer the blended spinach in a large bowl.
3. Add shredded provolone cheese, beaten egg, almond flour, and salt.
4. Stir the spinach mixture with the help of a spoon until it is homogenous.
5. Then make the patties from the spinach mixture.
6. Preheat the air fryer to 200°C.
7. Spray the air fryer basket with cooking spray from inside and put the spinach patties.
8. Cook them for 3 minutes and then flip on the other side.
9. Cook the patties for 3 minutes more or until they are light brown.

Green Beans and Tomato Sauce

Prep time: 5 minutes | Cook time: 15 minutes | Serves 4

- 225g green beans, trimmed and halved
- 160g black olives, pitted and halved
- 30g bacon, cooked and crumbled
- 1 tablespoon olive oil
- 60ml keto tomato sauce

1. In a pan that fits the air fryer, combine all the ingredients, toss, put the pan in the air fryer and cook at 190 degrees C for 15 minutes.
2. Divide between plates and serve.

Colorful Vegetable & Chicken Skewers

Prep time: 5 minutes | Cooking time: 10 minutes | Serves 4

- 300 g chicken breast fillet
- 200 g bacon
- 300 g tomatoes
- 300 g zucchini
- 300 g paprika
- 2 onions
- 100 g mushrooms
- 4 sprigs of thyme
- 2 sprigs of rosemary
- 6 tbsp olive oil
- Colorful pepper
- sea salt

1. Wash chicken breast and dab dry, then cut into even 2 cm cubes Peel the onion and cut into pieces.
2. Clean mushrooms and cut off the dry stem end Wash herbs and shake dry, then pluck the leaves from the stem and chop roughly.
3. Wash and drain the tomatoes and zucchini
4. Slice the zucchini Halve the peppers and then remove the seeds and partitions Wash the peppers and cut into pieces Cut the bacon into strips and roll up.
5. Place the prepared ingredients alternately on wooden skewers Place skewers on a plate and sprinkle with oil
6. Then season with salt and pepper and sprinkle with the herbs Grill in the air fryer.

Chives Lemon Chicory Mix

Prep time: 5 minutes | Cook time: 10 minutes | Serves 4

- 4 chicory heads, trimmed and halved
- Salt and black pepper to taste
- 1 tablespoon coconut oil, melted
- 1 tablespoon lemon juice
- ½ teaspoon nutmeg, ground
- 1 tablespoon chives, chopped

1. In a bowl, mix the chicory heads with the rest of the ingredients except the chives and toss well.
2. Put the chicory heads in your air fryer's basket and cook at 180 degrees Celsius for 10 minutes.
3. Divide the chicory between plates, sprinkle the chives on top and serve.

Vegetable Spring Rolls

Prep time: 10 minutes | Cooking time: 15 minutes | Serves 4

- ½ cabbage, grated
- 2 carrots, grated
- 1 tsp minced ginger
- 1 tsp minced garlic
- 1 tsp sesame oil
- 1 tsp soy sauce
- 1 tsp sesame seeds
- ½ tsp salt – 1 tsp olive oil
- 1 package spring roll wrappers

1. Combine all ingredients in a large bowl.
2. Divide the mixture between the spring roll sheets and roll them up; arrange on the baking tray.
3. Cook in the oven for 5 minutes on bake at 190°C (375°F).

Chickpea tomato & cucumber salad

Prep time: 5 minutes | Cooking time: 10 minutes | Serves 4

- 100 g tomatoes
- 50 g chickpeas
- 60 g cucumber
- 10 g spring onion
- 1 tbsp olive oil
- sea salt
- pepper

1. Wash tomatoes and cut into pieces Chickpeas in a colander and rinse under running water, then drain Wash cucumber and cut into pieces Clean spring onion and cut into rings.
2. Place tomatoes, chickpeas, cucumber, and spring onion in a salad bowl. Add olive oil and season with salt and pepper. Mix the salad and put in a bowl.

Kabocha Chips

Prep time: 15 minutes |Cook time: 11 minutes |Serves 2

- 6 oz Kabocha squash, peeled
- 1/2 teaspoon olive oil
- 1/2 teaspoon salt

1. Cut the Kabocha squash into thin chip-like slices and sprinkle with olive oil.
2. Preheat the air fryer to 200°C/ 392°F.
3. Place the Kabocha chips in the air fryer basket and cook for 5 minutes.
4. Then shake them well and cook for 6 minutes more or until they are crispy.
5. Sprinkle the cooked Kabocha chips with salt and mix well before serving.

Blooming Buttery Onion

Prep time: 10 minutes | Cooking time: 40 minutes | Serves 4

- 4 onions
- 4 knobs of butter
- 1 tbsp olive oil

1. Peel the onions and slice off the root bottom so they can sit flat.
2. Cut slices into the onion to make it look like a blooming flower, making sure not to go all the way through; four cuts should be enough.
3. Preheat the air fryer to 180°C (350°F) and place the onions in the basket.
4. Drizzle with olive oil, place a knob of butter on top of each onion and cook for about 30 minutes.
5. Serve with garlic mayonnaise dip.

Garlicky Vermouth Mushrooms

Prep time: 10 minutes | Cooking time: 20 minutes | Serves 3

- 907g portobello mushrooms, sliced
- 2 tbsp vermouth
- ½ tsp garlic powder
- 1 tbsp olive oil
- 2 tsp mixed herbs
- 1 tbsp duck fat

1. Add duck fat, garlic powder and mixed herbs in a food processor and blend until well combined.
2. Toss the mushrooms with olive oil and the herb mixture until well coated.
3. Preheat the air fryer to 350°F (180°C) and place the mushrooms in the basket.
4. Pour the vermouth over the mushrooms and cook for 10 minutes.
5. After 10 minutes, add more vermouth and cook for another 5-7 minutes until the mushrooms are tender and the liquid has evaporated.
6. Serve hot as a side dish or topping.

Chickpea & Halloumi Salad

Prep time: 5 minutes | Cooking time: 25 minutes | Serves 4

- 200 g chickpeas
- 200 g Halloumi
- 1 shallot
- ½ spring onion
- 30 g radish
- 50 g tomatoes
- 50 g paprika
- 50 g cucumber
- 20 g canned corn
- 4 stems of parsley
- 4 tbsp olive oil
- sea salt
- pepper

1. Place chickpeas in a sieve and rinse under running water, then drain.
2. Heat air fryer and fry halloumi on both sides until roast strips are recognizable
3. Season halloumi with salt and pepper, then remove from the air fryer and cut into pieces.
4. Meanwhile, clean the radishes and cut into thin slices. Wash tomatoes and cut into pieces. Deseed peppers and cut into pieces. Wash the cucumber and cut into small cubes.
5. Peel the shallot and cut it into fine rings. Clean the spring onion and cut into rings at an angle
6. Wash the parsley and shake it dry, then pluck the leaves and chop them Remove the corn from the can and drain.
7. Put all prepared salad ingredients in a bowl, and mix Add olive oil and some salt and pepper and stir again.

Steamed Veggies

Prep time: 5 minutes | Cooking time: 15 minutes | Serves 4

- 100 g broccoli
- 50 g paprika, red, fresh
- 50 g paprika, yellow, fresh
- 50 g onion
- 100 g snow peas, fresh
- 2 medium carrots, fresh
- 1 pinch of sea salt
- 1 tbsp olive oil

1. Wash the broccoli and cut the florets from the stalk Remove the peppers from the seeds and partitions and cut into strips.
2. Peel the onion and cut into rings Wash and drain the pears Peel the carrot and cut into thin sticks.
3. Heat the olive oil in the air fryer Put the prepared vegetables in the air fryer and fry them all over, stirring several times.
4. Season everything with salt and serve.

Chard, Avocado, Nut & Feta Salad

Prep time: 5 minutes | Cooking time: 15 minutes | Serves 4

- 20 g baby chard
- 60 g avocado
- 50 g dried tomatoes
- 30 g feta
- 30 g of walnuts
- 20 g red onion
- 2 tbsp olive oil
- sea salt
- pepper

1. Wash the chard and drain well. Halve the avocado and remove the seed, then peel the pulp and cut into small pieces.
2. Cut the dried tomatoes into pieces.
3. Crumble feta by hand. Chop walnuts. Peel onions and cut into rings.
4. Put all the ingredients and the olive oil in a salad bowl and mix. Finally, season the salad with salt and pepper and place on a plate.

Colorful Vegetable Salad

Prep time: 5 minutes | Cooking time: 25 minutes | Serves 4

- 1 eggplant, approx. 200g
- 150 g tomatoes
- 140 g paprika
- 50 g salad (endives, Roman, arugula)
- 1 small red onion
- ½ red chili pepper
- 2 cloves of garlic
- 4 tbsp olive oil
- cumin
- sea salt
- pepper

1. Wash eggplant and dry, then cut into pieces. Peel garlic and squeeze with garlic press. Mix eggplant with 1 tbsp olive oil, garlic, salt, and pepper in a bowl and spread on a baking sheet lined with parchment paper.
2. Cook eggplant for about 10 minutes at 160° C in a preheated air fryer.
3. Meanwhile, wash and quarter the tomatoes. Cut peppers into thin sticks. Wash lettuce leaves and shake dry, then cut into thin strips. Peel the onion and cut into strips. Cut chili pepper into thin rings.
4. Mix tomatoes, peppers, lettuce, onion, and chili pepper in a salad bowl. Add the olive oil, cumin, salt, and pepper and mix well.
5. Take the eggplant out of the air fryer, allow it to cool briefly and add to the salad. Mix everything and place on two plates.

Zucchini Chips

Prep time: 5 minutes | Cooking time: 20 minutes | Serves 4

- 400 g zucchini
- Bamboo salt
- pink pepper
- 2 tbsp olive oil

1. Wash the zucchini, dry them and cut off the ends Cut into very thin slices.
2. Place the zucchini slices on a baking sheet lined with parchment paper and salt.
3. Brush with olive oil.
4. Sprinkle the slices with paprika powder and lightly salt again.
5. Heat the zucchini slices in a 200° C preheated the air fryer for 8-12 minutes until golden brown.

Sweet Pear, Pomegranate & Nuts Salad

Prep time: 5 minutes | Cooking time: 10 minutes | Serves 4

- 1 small pear (about 100 g)
- 5 g baby spinach
- 30 pomegranate seeds
- 20 g walnuts

1. Wash and dry the pear, then cut in half and remove the core Cut the pear into thin slices Wash the spinach and drain well Chop the nuts roughly.
2. Layer the pear, spinach, pomegranate seeds, and walnuts alternately into a glass until all the ingredients have been consumed. Close the glass and refrigerate until ready to eat.

Smoothie Bowl with Spinach, Mango & Muesli

Prep time: 5 minutes | Cooking time: 10 minutes | Serves 4

- 150 g yogurt
- 30 g apple
- 30 g mango
- 30 g low-carb cereal (alternatively nuts, chopped)
- 10 g spinach
- 10 g Chia seeds

1. Wash spinach leaves and drain Peel mango and cut into strips Core the apple and cut into pieces.
2. Put the spinach, apple pieces and half of the mango strips with yogurt in a shaker Puree everything with the hand blender.
3. Put the spinach smoothie into a bowl Add low-carb cereal, chia seeds, and mango and serve.

Avocado & Mozzarella Salad Bowl

Prep time: 5 minutes | Cooking time: 10 minutes | Serves 4

- 60 g avocado
- 50 g tomatoes, colorful mixture
- 40 g mozzarella
- 30 g mixed salad
- 2 tbsp olive oil
- 1 stalk of basil
- sea salt
- pepper

1. Wash lettuce leaves and drain well, then chop into pieces and place in a bowl Wash tomatoes and slice Slice mozzarella Wash basil and shake dry, then peel off the leaves.
2. Halve the avocado and remove the core. Remove the avocado flesh from the skin and cut into strips. Add the avocado, tomatoes, mozzarella, and basil to the salad. Sprinkle with olive oil and season the salad bowl with salt and pepper.

Chapter 9
Dessert Recipes

Brownies

Prep time: 10 minutes | Cook time: 25 minutes | Serves 6

- 6 tablespoons soft cream cheese
- 3 eggs, whisked
- 2 tablespoons cocoa powder
- 3 tablespoons melted coconut oil
- ¼ cup almond flour
- ¼ cup desiccated coconut
- ¼ teaspoon baking powder
- 1 teaspoon vanilla extract
- ½ cup almond milk
- 3 tablespoons granulated sweetener
- Cooking spray

1. Grease a cake pan that fits your air fryer with cooking spray.
2. In a mixing bowl, combine the soft cream cheese, whisked eggs, cocoa powder, melted coconut oil, almond flour, desiccated coconut, baking powder, vanilla extract, almond milk, and granulated sweetener. Mix well.
3. Pour the mixture into the greased cake pan.
4. Place the pan in the air fryer basket and cook at 180°C/350°F for 25 minutes.
5. Remove from the air fryer and let cool. Cut into squares and serve.

Keto Butter Balls

Prep time: 15 minutes | Cook time: 10 minutes | Serves 4

- 1 tablespoon butter, softened
- 1 tablespoon Erythritol
- 1/2 teaspoon ground cinnamon
- 1 tablespoon coconut flour
- 1 teaspoon desiccated coconut
- Cooking spray

1. In a mixing bowl, combine the softened butter, Erythritol, ground cinnamon, coconut flour, and desiccated coconut.
2. Stir the mixture with a fork until it becomes homogeneous and forms a dough.
3. Divide the dough into 4 equal portions and roll each portion into a ball.
4. Preheat the air fryer to 375°F (190°C).
5. Spray the air fryer basket with cooking spray and place the balls inside.
6. Cook the butter balls in the air fryer for 10 minutes, or until lightly golden brown.
7. Remove the balls from the air fryer and allow them to cool for a few minutes before serving.

Avocado Cream Pudding

Prep time: m5inutes |Cook time: 25 minutes |Serving: 6

- 4 small avocados, peeled, pitted and mashed
- 2 eggs, whisked
- 240ml coconut milk
- 150g granulated sweetener (e.g. Erythritol)
- 1 teaspoon ground cinnamon
- ½ teaspoon ground ginger

1. In a bowl, mix all the ingredients and whisk well.
2. Pour the mixture into a pudding mold or oven-safe dish that fits your air fryer.
3. Preheat the air fryer to 175°C (350°F) and place the pudding in the air fryer basket.
4. Cook for 25 minutes.
5. Serve warm.

Walnuts and Almonds Granola

Prep time:4 minutes |Cook time: 8 minutes |Serves 6

- 1 cup avocado, peeled, pitted and cubed
- ½ cup coconut flakes
- 2 tablespoons butter, melted
- ¼ cup walnuts, chopped
- ¼ cup almonds, chopped
- 2 tablespoons sweetener (such as stevia)

1. In a bowl, mix the avocado, coconut flakes, melted butter, walnuts, almonds, and sweetener. Toss to combine.
2. Spread the mixture evenly in the air fryer basket.
3. Cook at 160°C (320°F) for 8 minutes, or until golden brown, stirring halfway through.
4. Remove from the air fryer and let cool completely.
5. Divide into bowls and serve immediately.

Cookies With Keto Marmalade

Prep time: 5 minutes | Cooking time: 25 minutes | Serves 6

- 3 eggs
- 70 g erythritol
- 160 g almond flour
- 1/2 tsp baking soda
- 1/2 tsp salt
- 60 g butter
- 50 g keto jam

1. reheat the air fryer to 180° C and line a baking sheet with parchment paper
2. Mix all ingredients (excluding keto jam) into a cookie dough
3. Place 12 cookies on the baking tray, flatten and press a spoon in the middle of the cookie dough
4. Fill with jam in the middle.
5. Bake the cookies and serve

Tasty Potatoes Au Gratin

Prep time: 10 minutes | Cooking time: 25 minutes | Serves 6

- 1 tsp. of black pepper
- 7 peeled Maris Piper potatoes
- 120 ml double cream
- 120 g grated semi-mature cheddar
- ½ tsp. of nutmeg
- 120 ml whole milk

1. Slice the peeled potatoes thinly.
2. Mix the milk and cream in a bowl. Season with nutmeg, salt, and pepper. Add the potato slices and toss until coated.
3. Arrange the coated potato slices in a baking dish.
4. Pour the seasoning mixture on top.
5. Bake in a preheated oven at 200°C (180°C fan) for 25 minutes.
6. Serve hot.

Hazelnut Vinegar Cookies

Prep time: 25 minutes | Cook time: 11 minutes | Serves 6

- 1 tablespoon flaxseeds
- ¼ cup flax meal
- ½ cup coconut flour
- ½ teaspoon baking powder
- 1 oz hazelnuts, chopped
- 1 teaspoon apple cider vinegar
- 3 tablespoons coconut cream
- 1 tablespoon butter, softened
- 3 teaspoons Splenda
- Cooking spray

1. Put the flax meal in the bowl.
2. Add flax seeds, coconut flour, baking powder, apple cider vinegar, and Splenda.
3. Stir the mixture gently with the help of the fork and add butter, coconut cream, hazelnuts, and knead the non-sticky dough.
4. If the dough is not sticky enough, add more coconut cream.
5. Make the big ball from the dough and put it in the freezer for 10-15 minutes.
6. After this, preheat the air fryer to 185C.
7. Make the small balls (cookies) from the flax meal dough and press them gently.
8. Spray the air fryer basket with cooking spray from inside.
9. Arrange the cookies in the air fryer basket in one layer (cook 3-4 cookies per one time) and cook them for 11 minutes.
10. Then transfer the cooked cookies on the plate and cool them completely.
11. Repeat the same steps with remaining uncooked cookies.
12. Store the cookies in the glass jar with the closed lid.

Keto Chocolate Mousse

Prep time: 5 minutes | Cooking time: 20 minutes | Serves 4

- 200 g dark chocolate min. 85%
- 90 ml water
- 3 eggs
- 50 ml coconut milk full fat
- 1 tbsp erythritol

1. Heat the chocolate together with the water and the erythritol in a water bath.
2. Stir until a smooth mass has formed. Then set aside.
3. Separate the eggs.
4. Stir the egg yolk and coconut milk into the chocolate mixture.
5. Beat the egg whites until stiff and fold gently.

Glazed Cherry Turnovers

Prep time: 10 minutes | Cook time: 56 minutes | Serves 8

- 2 sheets ready-rolled puff pastry, thawed
- 1 (21-ounce) can premium cherry pie filling
- 2 teaspoons ground cinnamon
- 1 egg, beaten
- 1 cup sliced almonds
- 1 cup icing sugar
- 2 tablespoons milk

1. Preheat the oven to 200°C/180°C fan/gas mark 6. Line a baking tray with parchment paper.
2. Roll out each sheet of puff pastry on a lightly floured surface to a square of approximately 30cm x 30cm. Cut each sheet into 4 equal squares.
3. Mix the cherry pie filling and cinnamon together in a bowl. Spoon ¼ cup of the cherry filling into the center of each puff pastry square. Brush the edges of the pastry with the egg wash. Fold one corner of the pastry over the cherry pie filling towards the opposite corner, forming a triangle. Seal the edges of the pastry together with the tines of a fork. Brush the top of the turnovers with the egg wash and sprinkle sliced almonds over each one.
4. Bake in the preheated oven for 20-25 minutes, or until the turnovers are golden brown and puffed up.
5. While the turnovers are baking, make the glaze by whisking the icing sugar and milk together in a small bowl until smooth. If the consistency is still too thick to drizzle, add a little more milk, a drop at a time, and stir until smooth.
6. Let the baked cherry turnovers cool for at least 10 minutes. Then drizzle the glaze over each turnover in a zigzag motion. Serve warm or at room temperature.

Fresh Cucumber Salad with Onions & Herbs

Prep time: 5 minutes | Cooking time: 10 minutes | Serves 4

- 200 g cucumber with shell, raw
- 15 g spring onion
- 2 stems of parsley, fresh
- 1 pinch of sea salt
- 1 pinch of pepper, black
- 1 tbsp olive oil

1. Wash cucumber and dry, then slice into thin slices, alternatively cut into thin slices with a knife.
2. Clean the spring onion thoroughly and cut into thin rings. Wash the parsley and shake it dry, then peel off the leaves and chop.
3. Put cucumber, spring onion and parsley with olive oil in a bowl and season with salt and pepper. Stir and serve.

Mediterranean Vegetable Omelet

Prep time: 5 minutes | Cooking time: 15 minutes | Serves 4

- 4 eggs
- 1 tbsp cream
- 4 cherry tomatoes
- 40 g paprika
- 50 g avocado
- 20 g peas, fresh or frozen
- 20g onion
- 20 g corn, canned
- 6 stalks of parsley
- 3 tbsp olive oil
- sea salt
- pepper

1. Wash and drain the tomatoes and peppers Slice the tomatoes, cut the peppers into thin strips Remove the avocado flesh from the shells and cut into strips Peel the onion and cut into thin strips.
2. Wash the parsley and shake it dry, then pluck the leaves from the stalk and chop them. Drain the corn in a colander.
3. Wash and drain the fresh peas, put the frozen peas in a bowl to thaw.
4. Pound the eggs in a bowl and whisk with cream, a little salt and pepper. Heat the oil in the air fryer and add the egg mass.
5. Distribute the prepared vegetables on the omelet and warm them.
6. Season with salt, pepper and sprinkle with parsley.
7. Carefully fold the omelet in half and place it on a plate.

Double Chocolate Cookies

Prep time: 8 minutes | Cooking time: 35 minutes | Serves 8

- Dough
- 150 g ground hazelnuts
- 1 tsp baking powder
- 1/8 tsp salt
- 20 g butter
- 45 ml walnut oil
- 60 g erythritol
- 1 egg
- 1/2 tsp vanilla flavor
- Filling
- 50 g dark chocolate 99% cocoa
- 30 g erythritol powdered sugar
- 35 g butter
- 1/4 tsp vanilla flavor

1. Preheat the air fryer to 160° C (circulating air) and prepare a baking tray with parchment paper.
2. Knead all ingredients for the cookie dough (preferably in a food processor) to a dough.
3. Spread 16 pastry blobs on the baking sheet with a tbsp and form into a round shape.
4. Bake the cookie dough in the air fryer for about 10 minutes, remove and allow it to cool well.
5. Melt bittersweet chocolate in a water bath.
6. Stir in butter, powdered sugar erythritol and vanilla flavor until smooth.
7. Spread the chocolate evenly over the cooled cookies.

Coconut Chocolate Fat Bombs

Prep time: 5 minutes | Cooking time: 2 hour 35 minutes | Serves 6

- 90 ml coconut oil
- 20 g cocoa butter
- 15 g baking cocoa
- 12 g Whey Protein Powder neutral
- 30 g erythritol
- 1/2 tsp almond extract

1. Melt the cocoa butter and coconut oil in a small air fryer on low heat.
2. Add the remaining ingredients and stir to a creamy mixture.
3. Pour these into ice cube or chocolate cases and place in the refrigerator for about 2 hours.
4. When they have become solid, squeeze out of the molds. Store in the refrigerator until consumption.

Keto Air Fryer Cakes

Prep time: 5 minutes | Cooking time: 10 minutes | Serves 4

- 3 eggs
- 80 g cream cheese

1. Mix the dough out of eggs and cream cheese (if available in a Food processor)
2. Bake in an air fryer (yield: 12 small air fryer cakes)

Low-Carb Carrot Cake

Prep time: 8 minutes | Cooking time: 55 minutes | Serves 6

- 5 eggs
- 200 g carrots
- 200 g butter
- 170 g cream cheese
- 100 g almond flour
- 30 g of walnuts chopped
- 20 g coconut flakes
- 4 ml erythritol
- 2 tsp baking powder
- 1 tsp cinnamon, ground
- 1 vial of vanilla flavor

1. Preheat the air fryer to 180° C.
2. Grate carrots.
3. Mix eggs, butter, 1 tbsp erythritol and vanilla flavor.
4. Add the grated carrots, walnuts, almond flour, baking powder and grated coconut and mix well.
5. Pour the cake dough into air fryer and bake for about 40 minutes.
6. Allow to cool.
7. Heat cream cheese in microwave for 20 seconds at medium power.
8. Mix the cream cheese with the remaining erythritol and spread over the cake.
9. Garnish with cinnamon.

Keto Chocolate Cake

Prep time: 5 minutes | Cooking time: 2 hours 25 minutes | Serves 6

- 300 g hazelnuts ground
- 60 g butter (soft)
- 3 tsp erythritol
- 1 pinch of salt
- 400 g mascarpone
- 200 g dark chocolate 99% cocoa
- 6 tsp erythritol
- 70 g butter (soft)
- 50 ml cream

OPTIONAL TOPPINGS:

- 150 ml cream
- garnish / refinement
- cocoa nibs
- cocoa powder

1. Preheat the air fryer to 180° C (convection).
2. Mix together butter, the ground hazelnuts, salt and erythritol and knead a cake dough
3. Lay out a springform air fryer (24 cm) with parchment paper
4. Distribute the dough evenly in the mold, press it flat and form a 1cm high edge
5. Bake the cake bottom for 15 minutes in the air fryer
6. Heat all ingredients for the cake topping at 40° C in the Cooking Chef and mix
7. Heat and liquefy mascarpone
8. Melt chocolate in a water bath
9. Mix the rest of the cake coating ingredients with mascarpone and chocolate
10. Spread the mixture on the cake and chill for 2 hours in the refrigerator
11. Then beat the cream for the topping stiff and spread on the chocolate cake
12. Garnish with cocoa powder and cocoa nibs

Lime Mousse

Prep time: 5 minutes | Cooking time: 2 hour 15 minutes | Serves 6

- 40 g egg yolk
- 40 ml lime juice or lemon juice
- 10 g erythritol
- 8 g gelatin powder
- 90 ml cream
- 1/4 tsp orange flavor

1. Beat the cream until stiff.
2. Separate the eggs and place the egg yolk in a small bowl. Use the egg white for another recipe.
3. Add erythritol to the egg yolk and stir well.
4. In a water bath, warm the lime juice and the orange flavors. Add the gelatin and stir until it dissolves. Stir in the egg yolks. Let cool down.
5. Carefully fold in the cream and spread on two glasses.
6. Put in the refrigerator for about 2 hours.

Appendix 1 Measurement Conversion Chart

Volume Equivalents (Dry)	
US STANDARD	METRIC (APPROXIMATE)
1/8 teaspoon	0.5 mL
1/4 teaspoon	1 mL
1/2 teaspoon	2 mL
3/4 teaspoon	4 mL
1 teaspoon	5 mL
1 tablespoon	15 mL
1/4 cup	59 mL
1/2 cup	118 mL
3/4 cup	177 mL
1 cup	235 mL
2 cups	475 mL
3 cups	700 mL
4 cups	1 L

Volume Equivalents (Liquid)		
US STANDARD	US STANDARD (OUNCES)	METRIC (APPROXIMATE)
2 tablespoons	1 fl.oz.	30 mL
1/4 cup	2 fl.oz.	60 mL
1/2 cup	4 fl.oz.	120 mL
1 cup	8 fl.oz.	240 mL
1 1/2 cup	12 fl.oz.	355 mL
2 cups or 1 pint	16 fl.oz.	475 mL
4 cups or 1 quart	32 fl.oz.	1 L
1 gallon	128 fl.oz.	4 L

Temperatures Equivalents	
FAHRENHEIT(F)	CELSIUS(C) APPROXIMATE)
225 °F	107 °C
250 °F	120 ° °C
275 °F	135 °C
300 °F	150 °C
325 °F	160 °C
350 °F	180 °C
375 °F	190 °C
400 °F	205 °C
425 °F	220 °C
450 °F	235 °C
475 °F	245 °C
500 °F	260 °C

Weight Equivalents	
US STANDARD	METRIC (APPROXIMATE)
1 ounce	28 g
2 ounces	57 g
5 ounces	142 g
10 ounces	284 g
15 ounces	425 g
16 ounces (1 pound)	455 g
1.5 pounds	680 g
2 pounds	907 g

Appendix 2 The Dirty Dozen and Clean Fifteen

The Environmental Working Group (EWG) is a nonprofit, nonpartisan organization dedicated to protecting human health and the environment Its mission is to empower people to live healthier lives in a healthier environment. This organization publishes an annual list of the twelve kinds of produce, in sequence, that have the highest amount of pesticide residue-the Dirty Dozen-as well as a list of the fifteen kinds ofproduce that have the least amount of pesticide residue-the Clean Fifteen.

THE DIRTY DOZEN	
The 2016 Dirty Dozen includes the following produce. These are considered among the year's most important produce to buy organic:	
Strawberries	Spinach
Apples	Tomatoes
Nectarines	Bell peppers
Peaches	Cherry tomatoes
Celery	Cucumbers
Grapes	Kale/collard greens
Cherries	Hot peppers
The Dirty Dozen list contains two additional itemskale/collard greens and hot peppers-because they tend to contain trace levels of highly hazardous pesticides.	

THE CLEAN FIFTEEN	
The least critical to buy organically are the Clean Fifteen list. The following are on the 2016 list:	
Avocados	Papayas
Corn	Kiw
Pineapples	Eggplant
Cabbage	Honeydew
Sweet peas	Grapefruit
Onions	Cantaloupe
Asparagus	Cauliflower
Mangos	
Some of the sweet corn sold in the United States are made from genetically engineered (GE) seedstock. Buy organic varieties of these crops to avoid GE produce.	

Appendix 3 Index

A
all-purpose flour 50, 53
allspice 15
almond 5, 14
ancho chile 10
ancho chile powder 5
apple 9
apple cider vinegar 9
arugula 51
avocado 11

B
bacon 52
balsamic vinegar 7, 12, 52
basil 5, 8, 11, 13
beet 52
bell pepper 50, 51, 53
black beans 50, 51
broccoli 51, 52, 53
buns 52
butter 50

C
canola oil 50, 51, 52
carrot 52, 53
cauliflower 5, 52
cayenne 5, 52
cayenne pepper 52
Cheddar cheese 52
chicken 6
chili powder 50, 51
chipanle pepper 50
chives 5, 6, 52
cinnamon 15
coconut 6
Colby Jack cheese 51
coriander 52
corn 50, 51
corn kernels 50
cumin 5, 10, 15, 50, 51, 52

D
diced panatoes 50
Dijon mustard 7, 12, 13, 51
dry onion powder 52

E
egg 14, 50, 53
enchilada sauce 51

F
fennel seed 53
flour 50, 53
fresh chives 5, 6, 52
fresh cilantro 52
fresh cilantro leaves 52
fresh dill 5
fresh parsley 6, 52
fresh parsley leaves 52

G
garlic 5, 9, 10, 11, 13, 14, 50, 51, 52, 53
garlic powder 8, 9, 52, 53

H
half-and-half 50
hemp seeds 8
honey 9, 51

I
instant rice 51

K
kale 14
kale leaves 14
ketchup 53
kosher salt 5, 10, 15

L
lemon 5, 6, 14, 51, 53
lemon juice 6, 8, 11, 13, 14, 51
lime 9, 12
lime juice 9, 12
lime zest 9, 12

M
maple syrup 7, 12, 53
Marinara Sauce 5
micro greens 52
milk 5, 50
mixed berries 12
Mozzarella 50, 53
Mozzarella cheese 50, 53
mushroom 51, 52
mustard 51, 53
mustard powder 53

N

nutritional yeast 5

O

olive oil 5, 12, 13, 14, 50, 51, 52, 53
onion 5, 50, 51
onion powder 8
oregano 5, 8, 10, 50

P

panatoes 50, 52
paprika 5, 15, 52
Parmesan cheese 51, 53
parsley 6, 52
pesto 52
pink Himalayan salt 5, 7, 8, 11
pizza dough 50, 53
pizza sauce 50
plain coconut yogurt 6
plain Greek yogurt 5
porcini powder 53
potato 53

R

Ranch dressing 52
raw honey 9, 12, 13
red pepper flakes 5, 8, 14, 15, 51, 53
ricotta cheese 53

S

saffron 52
Serrano pepper 53
sugar 10
summer squash 51

T

tahini 5, 8, 9, 11
thyme 50
toasted almonds 14
tomato 5, 50, 52, 53
turmeric 15

U

unsalted butter 50
unsweetened almond milk 5

V

vegetable broth 50
vegetable stock 51

W

white wine 8, 11
wine vinegar 8, 10, 11

Y

yogurt 5, 6

Z

zucchini 50, 51, 52, 53

AMY H. ANDERSEN

Printed in Great Britain
by Amazon